G000124029

THE 1922

By Philip Goodhart

In The Shadow of the Sword
Fifty Ships that Saved the World
The Hunt for Kimathi (with Ian Henderson)
War Without Weapons (with Christopher Chataway)
Referendum

THE 1922

The Story of the Conservative Backbenchers'
Parliamentary Committee

Philip Goodhart

with

Ursula Branston

MACMILLAN

© Philip Goodhart 1973

All rights reserved. No part of this publication
may be reproduced or transmitted, in any form or
by any means, without permission.

SBN 333 14386 8

First published 1973 by
MACMILLAN LONDON LIMITED
London and Basingstoke
Associated companies in New York Dublin
Melbourne Johannesburg and Madras

Printed in Great Britain by
NORTHUMBERLAND PRESS LTD,
Gateshead

Contents

Introduction

SOME TIME AGO, THE Chairman of a Conservative Meeting introduced me to the audience with the words, 'This is Mr Goodhart who is Secretary of the 1922 Committee, which is the Trade Union of Conservative back-bench MPs.' In a way, the Chairman was right, for the 1922 Committee does operate a closed shop, in that all back-bench Conservative Members of Parliament automatically become Members of the Committee and are entitled to attend the weekly meetings, held at six o'clock every Thursday evening. It is also true that in the fifty years of its existence, the 1922 Committee has spent more time discussing Members' pay than any other single topic – but unlike most other Trades Unions, most Members of the Committee have usually advised the Government not to increase parliamentary salaries. Meanwhile, there have been remarkably few threats of strike action from the Committee; for the withdrawal of support for the Conservative leadership is the ultimate weapon in the possession of any Conservative back-bencher.

As Robert McKenzie has written, in his volume *British Political Parties*:

> The 1922 Committee is in effect therefore an organization of the entire back-bench membership of the Conservative Party; it is intended to serve as a sounding board of Conservative opinion in the House of Commons, just as the National Union serves as a sounding board of Conservative opinion in the country. Neither the National Union nor the 1922 Committee is authorized to formulate policy for the party; neither do they control in any direct sense the activities of the Leader and his colleagues; both are intended merely to keep him informed of the state of

Conservative opinion. But there is this difference in the relationship of the Leader to the two organizations: the Leader must of course strive to win the confidence (and if possible the enthusiastic support) of the National Union if he is to lead his party to victory at the polls; but his position as Leader and ultimately as Prime Minister is solely and directly dependent on his ability to retain the confidence of the back-bench Conservative MPs who constitute the membership of the 1922 Committee.*

At another Conservative meeting, another Chairman introduced me by saying, 'As joint secretary of the 1922 Committee, Mr Goodhart helps to organise the most powerful pressure group in Parliament today.' This conspiratorial interpretation of the role of the 1922 Committee is sedulously fostered by sections of the press who enjoy giving the impression that the majority of committee members are preoccupied with a desire to flog the peasants and restore capital punishment for sheep stealing. As Professor Peter Richards has written in *Honourable Members*:

> Opponents of the Conservatives frequently allege that the 1922 Committee is the 'core of Tory reaction'; the impression is created of a body dominated by the most militaristic and extreme sentiments. It is often true that privacy is not an aid to moderation. Yet as all backbench Conservatives can attend the 1922 Committee, it can claim to be fully representative of opinion in the Party.†

In fact, the Committee's first Chairman was a Member who became a notably progressive Metropolitan Magistrate; and the topics which are supposed to arouse reactionary sentiments in right-wing bosoms – such as immigration and law and order – are rarely discussed. In fifty years, the 1922 Committee has discussed capital punishment at any length less than half a dozen times. But over the years, the pattern has remained the same. The main arguments about policy have been carried on in the specialist committees, while the 1922 Committee has

* Robert McKenzie, *British Political Parties*, p. 59 (Heinemann 1955).
† Peter G. Richards, *Honourable Members*, p. 99 (Faber 1959).

remained a forum to which Members could bring their fears and misgivings. In the late 1930s, the Committee was often preoccupied with the need for increasing the speed of re-armament. In the middle of the 1940s, it was fearful of the Party's loss of identity within the framework of the wartime coalition. Towards the end of the War, there were many voices raised in anger at the degree of toleration shown by the Coalition Government to the Communist take-over of Eastern Europe. In opposition there has been a lasting preoccupation with tactics which reached a climax of sorts after the General Election of 1950. At times a firm and largely unanimous expression of views within the 1922 Committee has helped the Government of the day to decide to change course. This happened in the fuel rationing controversy of 1942, and the television argument ten years later; but the main committee in general and the Executive Committee in particular have aimed at dialogue rather than confrontation with the leadership. The Executive of the 1922 Committee has some responsibility for seeing that there is also a continuing dialogue between the specialist groups within the Party.

The 1922 Committee was not the first of its kind in the field. On 12 February, 1906, the Parliamentary Labour Party elected its first officers and decided to hold weekly meetings of the whole party to discuss plans of campaign and, as the veteran Labour leader J. B. Clynes recalled, to 'set up committees to deal with outstanding questions'. In practice the Labour Party system of specialist committees does not seem to have emerged until the discussion of the Beveridge plans for post-war recon-struction began in 1943 and 1944.

The Liberal Party in its heyday had no equivalent to the Parliamentary Labour Party, but as Colin Coote, the former editor of the *Daily Telegraph* and a Coalition Liberal Member of Parliament from 1917 to 1922 has written:

The nearest thing to a Coalition Liberal Party Group was the New Members' Coalition Group of which I and, for a fleeting moment, Tom Mosley (!!) were Hon. Secretaries. This comprised about 150 MPs of both parties, Oscar Guest being the Liberal Chairman and Ernest Wild Conservative Chairman. The Group did not specialise in topics, but

finally concentrated on a vain effort to get Ll.G. and Bonar
to form a Centre Party.

The men who founded the 1922 Committee, then, were not
sailing on completely uncharted seas, but the speed and energy
which went into the formation of the specialist groups within
the 1922 Committee were quite unprecedented. Ever since the
Conservative Whips took a hand in the organisation of back-bench
specialist committees, the precise relationship between the 1922
Committee and the specialist groups has rarely been defined.
Fortuitously, the 1922 Executive is usually recruited from the
Chairman or Officers of the main specialist committees and
the Executive would rarely seek to intervene in a specialist field
unless it believed that adequate arrangements did not exist for
discussing some important topic. Thus, when the suggestion
was made, in the spring of 1972, that there should be a separate
Consumer Affairs Committee, informal discussions involving
the Ministers at the Department of Trade and Industry, the
Whips' Office and the 1922 Executive, were held before the
Committee was formally set up. When a Member of the 1922
Committee tells the Chairman or some other member of the
Executive that he wants to raise a topic at the main committee
meeting, he will normally be advised to raise it first in the relevant specialist committee. This reluctance to accept a topic for
discussion until it has been thrashed out in the specialist committee has meant that many of the issues which stirred most
controversy within the party were never fully discussed in the
1922 Committee itself.

Thus, the Empire Free Trade controversy and the Indian
Home Rule argument which threatened party unity so often in
the 1930s were hardly ever mentioned at the meetings of the
main committee while in the 1950s the fierce argument about
the policy of withdrawal from the Suez Canal Base largely
by-passed the 1922 Committee.

It must, therefore, be accepted that no history of the 1922
can pretend to be a complete history of the role of Conservative
back-benchers in the last fifty years. It would be an exaggeration
to say that issues rolled in and out of the Committee by chance,
but for every important topic discussed at a 1922 Committee
meeting there will be six that go undiscussed.

If there is a degree of chance about the way in which some issues come before the Committee, there are also many variations in the quality of the records of the Committee itself. The meetings of the Committee have almost invariably been 'off the record', and the quality of minute-keeping shown by successive secretaries has been of variable quality. As a historian I must deplore the inadequacy of the official minutes kept by the secretaries in the 1960s and 1970s. But by no means all the records have survived. I have talked to many Members of the Committee whose memory goes back far further than my own, but I have tried wherever possible to use the words of the minute books. It is often the practice of energetic Parliamentary Private Secretaries to write brief accounts of the more interesting meetings for their Ministers, and some of these have been given to me. When I have quoted from these accounts rather than the text of the minutes themselves, I have introduced the quotation with words such as 'A contemporary record says ...'

Generations of Conservative Members owe a great debt of gratitude to Ursula Branston for her matchless achievements as the principal expert in Foreign Affairs at the Conservative Research Department. Now the whole 1922 Committee has to acknowledge another debt of gratitude for her work on our records. I am personally grateful to Jane Marrin for her research work and to Betty Lias who had the impossible task of deciphering my handwriting.

PHILIP GOODHART

I

The Beginning
of the 1922

BY THE END OF World War I, Reginald Clarry had already built a respectable career as an engineer. Born in Derby in 1882, young Clarry had become an articled pupil in a gas works in London and had moved on swiftly to become manager of the Swansea Gas Co. and then managing director of the Duffryn Steel and Tin Plate Works. During the 1914-18 War he had worked in an advisory capacity at the Ministry of Munitions.

Politically, Reginald Clarry was a man of firm and even die-hard views. He was against Lloyd George. He was against the Coalition, and he was bitterly opposed to Conservative support for any administration headed by Lloyd George. On 13 October, 1922, after a brief campaign in which he had expounded his anti-coalition views with vigour, Reginald Clarry won the Newport by-election.

As an independent Conservative, Reginald Clarry had polled 13,513 votes. J. W. Bowen, the Labour candidate, received 11,425 votes, while Mr Lyndon Moore, an un-hyphenated Liberal who was the most pro-Coalition of all the candidates, was bottom of the poll with 8,841 votes.

'The country will see in this result a most complete condemnation of the Coalition Government' argued *The Times*, and that newspaper's verdict was underlined by Raymond Gibbs, the Conservative agent at Newport:

Our success was gained in the industrial vote. We got a great block of votes in exclusively working class districts. I saw the ballot-boxes opened, so I do not speak without evidence. The working classes have never understood the Coalition arrangement. The only hope for the Conservative Party is to get back onto straight party lines. Otherwise

three-fourths of the Conservative working men will drift
away from us ... It was not in the residential districts that
we polled so well yesterday. They went to the Liberal
candidate ...

I have known all along that the feeling of the rank and file
was that our party leaders have not been loyal to us ...
they have sunk the party principles in the maintenance of
the Coalition.

The timing of Mr Clarry's by-election victory was all important, for on the following day Conservative Members of Parliament were meeting at the Carlton Club to decide whether the
party should continue to support the Coalition. Austen Chamberlain, the leading Conservative advocate for a continuing
Coalition, advanced the argument that its maintenance was necessary if the Labour Party was to be beaten. Some of Austen
Chamberlain's points were challenged by Stanley Baldwin, but
the most convincing answer of all had already been provided by
Reginald Clarry's victory at Newport.

A decision to leave the Coalition was passed by 137 votes to
87. Within three hours the Government resigned.

At the General Election which soon followed, Conservative
candidates received 5,502,298 votes out of 14,392,330 cast, or
38.5% of the total poll, but with the opposition vote split
between the Liberals (2,668,143), the National Liberals
(1,412,772) and Labour (4,337,349) the Conservatives won 344
seats, while a further 42 Conservatives were returned unopposed.
This was enough to give the Conservatives an overall majority
of 100 over a divided opposition. Many of the Conservative
Members were entering Parliament for the first time.

The initiation of new Members to parliamentary life has its
austere side. The Chamber seems intimidating rather than
intimate; the neo-Gothic corridors and committee rooms afford
a cold welcome. Often it can be difficult for the individual,
even well-qualified and confident individuals, to find a role. It
is even more difficult for a back-bencher to find out what is
being planned at the top for subsequent endorsement below.
Politicians are usually gregarious by nature and it was not surprising that some of the new back-benchers should decide that
they might find their parliamentary feet more quickly if they

worked together. This meant forming a committee. On 18 April, 1923, a small group of new men met in Committee Room 8 of the House of Commons to discuss the formation of a Committee

> for the purpose of mutual co-operation and assistance in dealing with political and parliamentary questions, and in order to enable new Members to take a more active interest and part in Parliamentary life, it being clearly understood that it is the intention and desire of the Committee to render every assistance to the Government and the Party Whips in their efforts to carry on the affairs of the Nation upon the sound basis of Conservative principles.

A Resolution was carried at a resumed meeting on 23 April, the Officers and Executive were duly elected, and the Conservative Private Members (1922) Committee was declared open for business at 6 p.m. on Mondays (now Thursdays) throughout each Parliamentary session.

Reginald Clarry was present at the formation of this 1922 Committee, but the moving spirit was undoubtedly Gervais Rentoul, the new Member for Lowestoft.

At an early age Gervais Rentoul had developed formidable self-confidence and considerable histrionic powers. When he was still a comparatively junior boy at the City of London School, he won a prize for Shakesperian declamation.

> My greatest pleasure in the whole business was in being able to announce the good news to my father [a former Member of Parliament, who became a Judge at the Old Bailey]. I told him how we had been summoned into the room, one by one, to do our pieces before the headmaster, the elocution master, and a jury of sixth form boys, and that when we had all performed, we were called back into the room. The headmaster announced that, on this occasion, the judges were unanimous; and added that, although sometimes the competitors were so nearly matched it was difficult to make the award, this time one boy was so much better than the others that there had been no trouble in deciding.
>
> 'Then, of course, I knew I had won,' I said.
>
> 'Why was that?' asked my father quizzically, and was

much amused when I explained that although I realized I might possibly be beaten, no one else really could have been so much better than myself, as the headmaster had indicated.*

Gervais Rentoul's Oxford career was spectacular. A first in Jurisprudence was matched by the Presidency of the Union, but his major preoccupation was the Oxford University Dramatic Society. Contemporary reviews suggest that he was an Olivier among the University actors of his generation, and the redoubtable Herbert Tree urged him to become a professional and offered every assistance. Money, however, was not plentiful, and in April 1907 he was called to the Bar. Five years later he successfully defended Mrs Seddon in one of the most spectacular murder trials of the Edwardian era.

Early in 1922, Gervais Rentoul's wife read out a brief advertisement in the *Daily Mail*:

> Should this letter catch the eye of an honest, broad-minded imperialist, who is prepared to put his country before his party and to pay his own election expenses; who would scorn to be a mere monkey-on-a-stick to the Central Office of the Conservative Party; who has the pluck to refuse merely to raise his hand in voting every time at the imperious dictation of the leaders of the Party in power, without due regard to his own conscience or those whom he represents – then let him hasten to the Lowestoft Division of Suffolk, where an almost certain and safe seat is going 'begging' for the asking.

Rentoul replied, and some weeks later he received a postcard inviting him to an interview.

He was duly adopted, but was quickly warned by the Conservative Party's Chief Agent that he could expect no help at all from Central Office. It did not matter. On election day, Gervais Rentoul polled 3,000 votes more than the combined total of his National Liberal and Labour opponents. At the first formal meeting of the 1922 Committee he was elected Chairman.

Gervais Rentoul's fellow founders were also men with wide-ranging interests. The first Vice-Chairman was a Scotsman, Captain Clifford Charles Alan Laurence Erskine-Bolst, who had

* Gervais Rentoul, *This Is My Case*, p. 19 (Hutchinson 1944).

served in the Black Watch, married the daughter of an American Senator, and had been the Agricultural Adviser to the Principality of Wales, a breadth of experience that hardly seemed to match the interests of his constituents in Hackney.

Perhaps the most distinguished of the founding fathers was the newly-elected Treasurer, Sir John Hewett, GCSI, KBE, who had first gone out to serve in the North-Western Province in 1877. During an industrious and distinguished Indian career lasting thirty-four years, he had been Secretary to the Viceroy, Secretary to the Royal Commission on Opium in 1893, Chief Commissioner of the Central Provinces, Lieutenant Governor of the United Provinces, and President of the Coronation Durbar Committee. On his retirement in 1912, Sir John, who had the disconcerting habit of starting work at 4 a.m., divided his still formidable energies between the City and charitable work. The Dictionary of National Biography recalls that he was 'essentially an administrator and man of business with great driving force' and with 'an extraordinary power of disentangling the vital points of any problem from a mass of details'.

Sir John was 68 when he entered Parliament. Lord Titchfield, who had been serving with the Royal Horse Guards before his election, was forty years younger than Sir John, and as the Duke of Portland was the only member of the original Executive still alive at the fiftieth anniversary of the 1922 General Election.

Sitting with Lord Titchfield on the Executive was his former master at Eton, Annesley Somerville, who had gone to Eton as master of the Army Class in 1885. In his long scholastic career, Annesley Somerville had taught a fair proportion of the new recruits to the Conservative benches, but his interest had led him beyond classroom and common room into local political and local charitable works. He was honorary secretary of the Eton Workingmen's Allotment Society for almost fifty years. Somerville's taste for good works was matched by Kenyon Vaughan-Morgan, a governor of several London hospitals, who was elected joint Hon. Secretary of the first 1922 Executive with Reginald Clarry.

Indeed, the first Executive of the 1922 Committee seems to have been broadly representative of the dominant strands within the post-war Conservative Parliamentary Party. Colonel Ruggles-

Brise was a land-agent and farmer, who listed his hobbies as hunting, shooting and fishing. Sir Luke Thompson was an executive director of an important engineering company. Reginald Banks, KC, was a barrister of considerable eminence. Colonel Woodcock led a busy civic life as did Major James Edmondson who sat on the Oxfordshire County Council for fifteen years.

Only two members of the Executive represented seats north of Nottingham. Only one member, Annesley Somerville at Windsor, had a majority of 10,000. While eight had majorities of less than 5,000, two had majorities of less than 1,000.

Virtually all the members of the Executive of military age had seen extensive service during the War, but none had had quite as spectacular a career as Vice-Admiral Sir Guy Gaunt, who had been raised in the Australian Ballarat Goldfields where his father had been a magistrate. After running away from school to go kangaroo shooting, the ebullient Gaunt had sailed round the world as a Merchant Navy cadet in the old clipper ships, transferring to the Royal Navy at the age of 19 with a Second Mate's certificate. Guy Gaunt gravitated naturally towards trouble and the most spectacular episode in his early career came in Samoa where, largely on his own initiative, he recruited a motley bunch of islanders known as Gaunt's Brigade to put down a tribal rebellion against the Samoans who were co-operating with the American, German and British representatives.

In May 1914, Guy Gaunt had gone to Washington as Naval Attaché, and on the outbreak of war he had thrown himself into intelligence work with gusto. In Washington he was a close friend of Franklin Roosevelt, then the American Assistant Secretary of the Navy, and had a valuable entrée to the White House, but the part of the war which he recalled with most relish was a lonely dash round the jungles of Venezuela, Colombia and Surinam, trying to put German wireless stations out of action.

Guy Gaunt clearly revelled in his Bulldog Drummond–James Bond role, but at the end of the War he was unemployed and a rash speculation in American property left him badly in need of a job. Admiral Hall, his old commander in Naval Intelligence, helped to secure Guy Gaunt's adoption for the supposedly radical seat of Buckrose in the East Riding where his boisterous

electioneering style helped him to ride a Conservative tide into
the House.

Once in the House, Guy Gaunt was one of those most in
favour of some organisation to help new members. This is how
he recalled the situation:

> What struck me on first getting into the House is that a
> man goes there, probably one of the most difficult positions
> in the world, and has to explain later on to many thousands
> of his constituents intricate problems of which he knows
> practically nothing. At every other profession a man has
> had some previous training. In Committee Room 14 of the
> House I held forth on this subject to a party of the newly
> elected members, and found that they all agreed with me.
>
> There was a by-election at Burnley. I went down to help
> and had a very rough ride. Back in the House several
> members came up and said: 'We have arranged that you
> shall see the Prime Minister this evening to put forward
> your views on educating members.'
>
> The Prime Minister was very attentive as I urged that
> we didn't want a partnership, but we did want a kinder-
> garten when there was an important Bill before the House.
> The Minister concerned might give us an hour clearly
> explaining it. Under the present system all we knew of the
> intricacies of the Bill was that a Whip said: 'We're voting
> Aye or No', as the case might be.*

Naturally it was a particular concern of the new Committee
to establish a good working relationship with the Whips. The
Committee was also anxious to try and maintain the confidential
nature of its meetings. It was noted in the minutes of one of the
first meetings that there should be 'no communication of the
proceedings to any persons not members of the Conservative
Party in the House of Commons'. The press however was already
curious, and the same early minute records that 'in view of the
repeated appearance in the *Yorkshire Post* of a statement
reflecting on the intentions of the Committee, the Chief Whip
should be consulted', and that the advisability of taking any

* Admiral Sir Guy Gaunt, *The Yield of the Years*, p. 282 (Hutchinson
1940).

step to deal with such reports should be left to the Chairman
or his Deputy.

The Chief Whip, Colonel Leslie Wilson, attended the first
regular meeting. He might have been expected to counsel
masterly inactivity rather than Private Members' enterprise; but
Colonel Wilson was not a Chief Whip in the orthodox mould.
He had only entered Parliament a year before the beginning of
the War, and at the Carlton Club meeting he had shrugged off
the normal reticence of the Whips' Office to make a powerful
speech against the Coalition. Within three months of the establishment of the 1922 Committee he was to leave the House and
become Governor of Bombay.

In fact, he offered co-operation as well as words of caution.
His attitude may have been motivated by enlightened self-interest
on behalf of the Whips, for the Committee was rapidly gaining
ground and expanding its membership to include older Members,
not elected for the first time in 1922. It was not long before the
attendance of a Whip to announce the business for the forthcoming week had become a regular practice; he did not, however,
take part in the Committee's general proceedings. Among
courteous exchanges in those early days was a request from the
Chief Whip that the Committee should make itself responsible
for the attendance of three Members prepared to carry on the
debate, if necessary, between 8 and 10 p.m. (the dinner hour)
each Tuesday. The Committee agreed, though the novelty soon
began to wear off judging by later difficulties in finding volunteers and pleas for longer notice of what was to be debated.

As a Secretary of the Committee, Reginald Clarry seems to
have borne more than his fair share of this chore. In 1923 he
seems to have addressed the House on more than twenty
occasions, on such diverse subjects as Ireland, income tax, naval
pensions, rents, and the future of the coal industry. Perhaps
the most important meeting of the Committee's infancy was
held on 2 May, 1923. At that meeting it was decided to form a
number of specialist sub-committees to discuss Government
policies in greater detail. The minutes also record that 'A letter
was received from Mr S. Roberts (Hereford) enquiring whether
membership of this Committee is available for all Members of
the Party; after consideration it was decided that the names of
any "older" Members of the Conservative Party (i.e. those not

elected for the first time to this present Parliament) who may express a desire to join the Committee should be considered by the Committee.' Mr Roberts was duly elected and after this a steady stream of applications from 'older' Members was approved. It was an all-important decision, for if 'older' Members had been excluded the Committee would certainly have withered and died – as other informal groups of newly-elected Members have eventually withered away.

While the 1922 Committee was finding its feet, the Prime Minister, Stanley Baldwin, was becoming increasingly convinced that there could be no revival of British industry or cure for unemployment without the introduction of a much wider measure of tariff reform than anything yet contemplated by the Conservative Administration. This was not altogether surprising, for Stanley Baldwin had made his maiden speech on tariff reform and Stanley Baldwin's father had been a fervent supporter of Joseph Chamberlain's tariff-reform campaign. There was, however, one major hurdle to the adoption of a full-blown tariff policy; at the 1922 General Election Bonar-Law, as Leader of the Party, had given a pledge that there would be no fundamental fiscal change during the lifetime of the next Parliament. Ill-health had removed Bonar-Law from politics, but it had not removed his pledge.

Stanley Baldwin's decision that he must be free to adopt a tariff reform policy seems to have been taken in the first week of October, at the beginning of the Imperial Economic Conference. Unemployment was still rising. Exports had reached a bare 70% of their pre-war volume. The Dominion Prime Ministers were calling for a guaranteed market in Great Britain, and the European economic scene seemed chaotic. On 5 October, Stanley Baldwin revealed his belief that he must now seek absolution from Bonar-Law's pledge to Neville Chamberlain, the Chancellor of the Exchequer. On 8 October the Chairman of the Conservative Party was warned that a General Election was imminent. On 23 October, Stanley Baldwin outlined his tariff proposals to the Cabinet. He argued that the whole economic system of Europe had broken down and that there was only one way to fight unemployment and that was to protect the home market against foreign manufacturers. More than half the Cabinet already knew what was in Stanley Baldwin's mind, but there was substantial opposition from the 'free trade' members of the Cabinet. Some other ministers were alarmed by the prospect of an early General Election, but broadly the Cabinet acquiesced, and on 25 October Stanley Baldwin addressed the Conservative Party Conference at Plymouth. He described unemployment as 'the crucial problem of our country'. He told the Conference:

> If I can fight it, I am willing to fight it. I cannot fight it without weapons ... if we go on pottering along as we are we shall have grave unemployment with us to the end of time, and I have come to the conclusion myself that the only way of fighting this subject is by protecting the home market.

At the time it seems that Stanley Baldwin had looked forward to an educational campaign on the tariff issue lasting for several months before he called a General Election. But once it became clear that an election was bound to come within six months, election fever mounted quickly. In the middle of November Baldwin decided on an immediate election. Both wings of the Liberal Party and the Labour Party campaigned on the issue of food taxes and fears of a higher cost of living. The country voted on 9 December. The result was: Conservatives 257 seats, Labour 191, Liberal 158. The Conservatives won 18 seats but lost 67 seats to the Liberals and 40 to the Labour Party. When the results were in, *The Times* reported 'The general opinion in Unionist circles yesterday was that Mr Baldwin's policy had been defeated on the "dear food cry".' In January 1924 Mr Ramsay Macdonald became Prime Minister at the head of a Labour Government which was dependent on Liberal support.

The 1922 Committee was not amused by this result. Four members of the Executive, Erskine-Bolst, Ruggles-Brise, Hewett and Woodcock, had been defeated while the survivors had generally had to find their own election expenses – which then ran to about £1,000 per member – for a contest which many Members believed could have been avoided. Naturally there was a demand that ordinary Members should be consulted more often when it came to policy-making and party strategy.

The first move made by the Committee after the election was the setting up of an Executive sub-committee whose brief was to obtain the opinions of all past and present members of the full Committee 'as to the reasons in each constituency underlying the defeat and reduced majorities of Conservative candidates'. Meanwhile a Resolution was passed expressing the Committee's 'regret' that steps were not taken to consult the Committee upon any new Government policy prior to the General Election. A special meeting was held early in February outside the House of Commons at which ex-Members who had been defeated were also present. At the conclusion of the meeting two Resolutions were carried. The first endorsed Mr Baldwin's retention of the Leadership. The second expressed the Committee's 'emphatic conviction' that the Party, at this critical juncture, should take steps to place its organisation on a democratic basis and to establish a closer contact between the Leader and the rank-and-file, and that for this purpose 'a Committee fully representative of the Party should be appointed'.

These Resolutions were sent to the Chief Whip and to the Party Chairman. But the dust had not yet settled, and it was decided, when the Committee met again in the House, to invite the Chief Whip and the Party Chairman to another special meeting, specifically to discuss the holding of regular Party meetings open to all Conservative MPs. The party leaders were also to be sent copies of the sub-committee's report on the reasons for the recent electoral defeat.

The preamble of this document said that it represented the views of 65 present members of the 1922 Committee and of some 40 former members, and was based on six fuller reports from members of the last Parliament who were defeated, and eleven from members who had held their seats, but usually with reduced majorities. The sorest point, of course, was the rushed way in which Protection had been introduced as the theme:

In the first place, there is a concensus of opinion that the issue at the Election and the moment chosen for forcing it were mainly responsible for the reverse sustained. While Protection is undoubtedly popular among those who believe in it and understand it, there are many in the Party who are by no means convinced that it is a policy that can be

adopted with advantage to the country ... The circumstances of the last Election, and the short time allowed
for the development of the policy, and for the propaganda
work, rendered it quite impossible to explain the policy in
such a way as to remove existing suspicions. The fact that
some of our candidates genuinely opposed Protection, but
fought for the Party because at short notice they could not
be replaced, naturally weakened the prospects of those who,
side by side with them, were fighting as whole-hearted
supporters of the Party policy. There is a general opinion
that no policy inconsistent with pledges given at a previous
Election should be brought forward as the policy of the
Party without further consideration with the rank-and-file
and those who advise the Party in the constituencies ...

Other and lesser factors militating against success, the report
suggested, were the unpopularity of rent restriction and the lack
of time for the country to feel the remedial effect of the Government's housing legislation. But the chief criticism was reserved
for the failure of the Party organisation to adapt its approach
to the changed nature of the electorate following the extension
of the franchise:

The enormous additions to the electorate have altered the
whole position of organization, and the existence of a large
body of electors possessing unformed or no political
opinions has emphasised the difficulties to which that
increase has given rise. In former days, by organization it
was possible to keep in touch with the trend of political
thought, but a much wider scheme of organization will be
necessary if efficient work is to be done.

Finally, there is a certain prophetic note in the reference to the
potential value of women in propaganda work and canvassing:

Women, if properly instructed and interested, are a great
force, but at present, and particularly on an occasion like
the recent Election, they were largely uninstructed and
consequently uninterested and timorous. They were, therefore, the easy prey of unscrupulous misrepresentation.

On 27 February, at Mr Baldwin's invitation, a deputation from the 1922 Committee consisting of the Chairman (Mr Rentoul), Deputy Chairman (Col. Vaughan Morgan), Secretary (Mr R. Clarry), Sir Guy Gaunt, Sir Douglas Newton, and Major Davies, waited upon him in his room at the House. Gervais Rentoul has written his own description of the interview:

> The demand we ventured to put forward was for regular Party meetings, under the chairmanship of the Leader, or some deputy appointed by him, at which from time to time an indication would be given to the rank and file of the general policy of the Party, and an opportunity afforded to members to raise any questions or points that seemed to them of importance. We complained of being left too much in the dark regarding the purposes and policy of the Government, which ultimately we, as private Members, would have the responsibility of supporting and fighting for in the constituencies, and pointed out that such a state of affairs could only lead to weakness and confusion.
>
> Mr Baldwin, when replying, said that he fully sympathized with the feelings expressed, and added that he had shared them himself during the many years when he was also a private Member. He felt, however, that Party meetings would be a mistake, mainly because of the inevitable leakage to the Press. Sir Austen Chamberlain also deprecated the idea, on the ground of lack of secrecy and because it might merely lead to schisms in the Party. To this we retorted that it might be the means of preventing schisms developing.
>
> But although sticking to our guns as long as possible, we had finally to beat a retreat, being finally flattened out by the remark from Sir Austen that we must trust our leaders, and that when we had been longer in the House, we would take a different view. Mr Baldwin also added, rather hopefully, that many similar bodies to the '1922' Committee had been started in the past and had in a short time disappeared. The deputation had, therefore, to withdraw, entirely unconvinced, content with the compromise that one of the Whips would in future attend all meetings

of the Committee and report direct to the Leader any views that might be expressed thereat.*

In giving an account of what had passed, the deputation could only report to their fellow Committee members that 'Unfortunately, for the moment, the object of the interview has not been achieved'. Nevertheless a noteworthy initiative had been taken. There were no hard feelings. Less than three weeks later, on 18 March, Mr Baldwin was guest of honour at the first dinner given by the Committee.

However, Mr Rentoul and his colleagues remained alert to any suggestions of encroachment on the 'special status', as they saw it, of the 1922 Committee. This came to the fore in the matter of the senior Committee's relationship with the newly-formed party group committees.

These had sprouted like dandelions after the setback at the General Election. Different party leaders had different motives for encouraging their growth. At one level Neville Chamberlain, who founded the Conservative Research Department, was anxious to get party groups formed so that policies could be discussed and hammered out in detail. He saw the development of party groups as a stepping-stone to a better informed party. Meanwhile, the new Chief Whip was Commander Bolton Meredith Eyres-Monsell, who had first gone to sea as a Midshipman in 1896, and knew that an idle crew was likely to make trouble, while a crew that was busy keeping everything shipshape was unlikely to be mutinous. He saw the development of the party group system as a means of filling empty hours.

The 1922 Committee considered it must be kept informed of any important actions or decisions these groups might take, and that this could most conveniently be done by receiving regularly brief reports from its own designated representatives who were also members of the particular party groups. Gervais Rentoul argued that, while the establishment of the group committees was welcome as far as it went, that still left a positive need for a clearing-house in order that Members might know the mind and policy of the Party on all the various subjects dealt with by the group committees.

* Gervais Rentoul, *Sometimes I Think*, pp. 234-5 (Hodder & Stoughton 1940).

A senior Whip, Captain Hacking, was invited to give his views. He emphasised that the Whips' Office were not antagonistic to the 1922, but were anxious about the confidential aspect of the group committees' reports. To that end he suggested that the consent of each group's chairman should first be obtained and there should be no circulation of written minutes. This procedure was submitted to the Party leaders, approved and put into effect in April. Only the Chairman of the Foreign Affairs Committee is on record as having reservations, informing the 1922 that he objected to any report being made until he had fully considered the matter. But, in practice as well as principle, the special status of the 1922 Committee had been recognised and enhanced.

From these relatively parish pump affairs, the Committee turned its attention to the increasingly urgent prospect of forcing a General Election.

The election battle was joined in October 1924 and the result was decisive. The Conservative vote went up by two million, to seven and a half million, which produced 415 seats. The Labour Party vote rose to five and a half million votes, but they won only 152 seats. The greatest losses, however, were suffered by the Liberals. Their strength in the House of Commons was cut to 47 seats.

In November, Mr Baldwin formed his second Conservative Ministry with an absolute majority of 222. Mr Winston Churchill was elected for Epping as a 'Constitutionalist' with a 10,000 majority (he would not at that time adopt the name Conservative), and he was at once invited by Mr Baldwin to accept office as Chancellor of the Exchequer. A year later, to quote Mr Churchill, 'with the approval of my constituents, and without being pressed personally in any way, I formally rejoined the Conservative Party'.

The first great policy dispute involving the Committee came in the early months of 1925, over the best means to deal with what was widely regarded as the abuse of the trade union political levy – the system under which part of a trade union member's subscription was paid into a special fund to be used for political purposes. In practice this money provided the principal financial support for the Labour Party. A Cabinet Committee had been appointed to enquire into the working of

the political levy, when its work was overtaken by the introduction of a Private Member's Bill. The Bill, the initiative of a
Scottish Conservative member, Mr Frederick Macquisten, aimed
to amend the law of 1913 which permitted Trade Unions to
impose a political levy which individuals could only avoid by
'contracting out' – a complicated system that involved some
effort on the part of all concerned. Mr Macquisten wanted to
change the system on the grounds that it was not right to ask
trade unionists for a political levy of which they might dis-
approve. His Bill had strong backing in the 1922 Committee:
a vote taken at a special committee meeting on 25 February
showed 40 in favour of the Bill as against 16 preferring to await
the results of the Government inquiry before pressing for
legislation.

Immediately after the 1922 Committee meeting, a deputation
called on the Prime Minister to tell him of the Party's views.

It seems that a majority of the Cabinet, including Neville
Chamberlain and Winston Churchill, were also in favour of the
Bill, but Stanley Baldwin was determined not to have a show-
down with the trades unions on that issue at that time.

The Bill was debated on 6 March. It was not surprising that
at a meeting of the Committee a few days before, the Whip,
Captain Hacking, again urged members to keep an open mind
until they had heard the Prime Minister's statement in the debate.
Some members remarked that the Press appeared to have been
informed of the Government's attitude before it was made
known to MPs.

Stanley Baldwin intervened in the debate with a remarkable
plea for industrial peace:

> We find ourselves in possession of perhaps the greatest
> majority our Party has ever had, and with the general assent
> of the country. Now how did we get there? It was not by
> promising to bring this Bill in; it was because, rightly or
> wrongly, we succeeded in creating an impression throughout
> the country that we stood for stable Government and for
> peace in the country between all classes of the community ...
>
> That being so, what should our course be at the begin-
> ning of a new Parliament?
>
> I want my Party today to make a gesture to the country,

and to say to them: 'We have our majority; we believe in the justice of this Bill which has been brought in today, but we are going to withdraw our hand, and we are not going to push our political advantage home at a moment like this. Suspicion which has prevented stability in Europe is the one poison that is preventing stability at home, and we offer the country today this: we, at any rate, are not going to fire the first shot. We stand for peace. We stand for the removal of suspicion in the country. We want to create an atmosphere, a new atmosphere in a new Parliament for a new age, in which the people can come together. We abandon what we have laid our hands to. We know we may be called cowards for doing it. We know we may be told that we have gone back on our principles. But we believe we know what, at this moment, the country wants, and we believe it is for us in our strength to do what no other Party can do at this moment, and to say that we at any rate stand for peace.'

The 1922 Committee, meeting before the Division, accepted the Prime Minister's argument – though maintaining the need for eventual legislation – and Mr Macquisten withdrew his Bill. That the affair had been painful was evident from the hope expressed by Mr Clarry, the Committee's Secretary, at the next meeting 'that the Whips would not put such a strain on the loyalty of members again'.

Reaction in the Committee to Mr Churchill's first Budget on 21 April, 1925 (6d off income tax, slight relief in super tax but increased death duties, together with old age pensions at sixty-five and pensions for widows and children) was quiet enough and there were no further controversies in the Committee before the end of the session.

Returning to the House after the summer recess, the Committee followed what had become a customary practice at their first meeting of a general discussion on the state of opinion in the constituencies. The chief source of discontent appeared to be the Rating and Valuation Bill, but the discussion led on to the broad question of national economic policy. From this followed a Resolution to form a sub-committee 'with a view to preparing practical suggestions for national economy to be submitted to the Treasury'. This was to bear some surprising fruit.

At the end of the year the Committee's membership was 185. From this substantial position the Chairman felt justified in sounding out the Chief Whip's view on the possible enlargement of the Committee next session by inviting all Private Members to join, dropping '1922' from its title, and including on the Whip notices of the Committee's weekly meetings. These proposals, however, did not please the Committee members, who voted in favour of retaining '1922' in their title, and were opposed to prejudicing the Committee's unofficial character, and perhaps its independence, by a notice on the Whip. But it was agreed to invite all Private Members to join.

By now the form of the regular meetings followed a set pattern. The Executive met to draw up the agenda immediately prior to the full Committee; the Chairman opened the proceedings; a Whip attended to outline the week's Business and to answer any questions about it; brief reports of the activities of party groups were given by the 1922 representatives appointed to them; a discussion followed on any special policy issue brought forward by the Executive or by a Private Member's initiative, or the meeting was addressed by an invited guest – often a Minister – who could be freely questioned. These Ministerial excursions sometimes produced press leaks, but it was not until 1928 that the Executive found it necessary to check, or attempt to forestall, the probings of the press by drafting agreed statements at the conclusion of important meetings.

The subjects discussed ranged from the broadest sweep of national policy to the smallest detail of House of Commons life. Thus, in the space of a few weeks, Mr Penny raised the question of the annual collection by the Whips for the Police and Messengers in which he understood the 'badged men' did not participate, and asking if they could be included; Major Tasker voiced the age-old difficulty of being called by the Speaker; Mr Peto criticised the arrangements for the comfort of Members in the Library, and the generally inadequate accommodation in the House; there was a call from Mr Campbell that Members should volunteer for the Special Constabulary; Major Cohen and Captain Ian Fraser, both severely wounded in the war, led a discussion on the need for much more liberal treatment of disabled ex-service pensioners and especially of neurasthenic cases.

The 1922 Committee was alive and well and an established part of the Westminster scene.

2

From Strike to Slump
(1925-31)

WHILE THE 1924-25 SESSION had ended quietly for the Committee, the 1925-26 Session was stormy enough for the most combative politician.

Stanley Baldwin failed in his attempt to lay the foundations of industrial peace; and on 6 May, 1926, the 1922 Committee met to hear the Chairman announce that during the General Strike the Committee would meet daily from Monday to Thursday. After that, Members listened to Lord Eustace Percy (acting as liaison between the House and the Government Intelligence Department), and adopted the following Resolution at the close of the meeting:

> The Members of the 1922 Committee desire to express to the Prime Minister their deep sympathy with him and entire approval of his action in making, in spite of the threat of a General Strike, a firm stand for the maintenance of ordered Government and the rights and power of Parliament as guardian of the liberties of the people.
>
> They further assure him that he may rely on their unqualified support in refusing to negotiate in the coal dispute until the General Strike is called off.

There was not much for back-benchers to do during the emergency and the Government suggested that members with industrial constituencies much affected by the strike might go to their constituencies and seek to rally public opinion.

A week later, on May 12, at a large meeting (116 members were present) the Committee heard a brief statement by the Chairman on the unconditional ending of the Strike. A general discussion was in progress – including questions such as the need now to introduce Trade Union legislation, and the scope

of the Government's guarantee of protection for non-strikers –
when, to quote from the record: 'The Secretary of State for War
and the Chief Whip entered the room, and Sir Lamington
Worthington-Evans read a transcript of the shorthand notes of
the meeting between the Prime Minister and the Trade Union
Council, which he announced would be broadcast that evening
and published in the press tomorrow.'

But clearly this was not the end of the story, and there was
widespread feeling on the back-benches that industrial relations
must be brought within the framework of the law. This was
taken up at the meeting on 17 May, during the discussion
of a motion by Sir Alfred Hopkinson, that the 1922 should set
up a sub-committee to report on the whole question of Trade
Union legislation. Not all members concurred. Doubts were
expressed whether the moment was opportune; many members
argued that a 'cooling-off' period should come first. It was agreed
to postpone further discussion until after the Whitsun recess.

When the 1922 resumed the discussion, the Committee was
reminded that the Government's own Cabinet Committee on
Trade Union legislation was still discussing the problem. Sir
Alfred Hopkinson protested that his proposal for an investigation was not an attempt to dictate to the Government, nor
was it an attack on Trade Unions as such; the object was to
help, not hinder, better industrial relations. On this basis the
motion gathered support (among the supporters was Captain
Oliver Stanley), and the Home Secretary (Mr Joynson Hicks)
was invited to address the Committee. After a résumé of the
work so far of the Cabinet Committee on Trade Union legislation, he assured members that the Government was anxious
to get the opinions of the Party and therefore of the 1922
Committee. A Resolution was then put in the following terms
and carried by a large majority:

> This Committee being of opinion that Trade Unions are
> an essential part of our industrial organisation and being
> anxious to support them, but considering that the difficulties
> of the whole subject require careful and sympathetic
> investigation, appoints a sub-committee consisting of six
> members, with power to add to their number, to consider
> the subject and to make such suggestions, if any, as it feels

can safely be made within such time as may be available. The members of the sub-committee to be selected by the Executive.

They were Sir Leslie Scott (who soon became Solicitor-General), Mr Greaves-Lord, Mr Sandeman-Allen, Mr Cyril Lloyd, Mr Luke Thompson and Mr Rentoul. Captain Harold Macmillan was soon added to their number.

The chief points suggested for possible reform of Trade Union legislation were the registration of Unions, compulsory conciliation machinery, secret ballot, and regulations to govern picketing. With the summer recess imminent, it was sensibly proposed that Members should sound out their constituents' reactions to these suggestions, but without mentioning their source. This was done, with the result that, when the Committee returned in November, a strongly-worded Resolution was carried unanimously and sent to the Prime Minister:

This Committee having regard to the strong feeling expressed in the constituencies considers it vital in the interests of the country and of trade unionism that firm and definite action dealing with the present abuses in Trade Union practice and defects in Trade Union Law affecting the liberty of the subject and of individual trade unionists should be taken without delay, and looks to the Government for a clear and positive pronouncement before the end of the present session as to their intended course.

To this, Harold Macmillan moved an addendum dealing with industrial reform, conciliation and arbitration, but agreed to withdraw it and to raise the question at a future meeting. It was, in fact, raised as a Resolution, seconded by Mr R. S. Hudson:

This Committee earnestly hopes that the Government will formulate and carry into law by progressive steps a wide and far-reaching industrial policy, comprising facilities for the spread of industrial co-operation in all its forms, coupled with the introduction of statutory machinery for arbitration and conciliation suited to the varying needs of different industries.

The discussion on Captain Macmillan's motion was twice

interrupted by Divisions, and was then adjourned. The discussion was indeterminate, and nothing further appears to have been heard of this particular initiative, but the 1922 sub-committee kept in close touch with the Cabinet sub-committee.

The Trade Disputes Bill, embodying many of the recommendations of the 1922 sub-committee, began its stormy passage through the Commons early in May 1927, and became law in July. In the course of his speech in the debate, Mr Baldwin raised an echo of the 1925 controversy over the withdrawal of Mr Macquisten's Bill. He explained that he had not then wanted it to appear that the Conservatives were 'firing the first shot' in a struggle with the Unions, but now on the basis of the events of the past year, there could be no doubt the Government had a mandate.

The Government also had a mandate for extending the right to vote to all women over the age of 21. In the 1924 Election campaign, Stanley Baldwin had given a pledge that the Party was in favour of 'equal political rights for men and women, and they desire that the question of the extension of the franchise should, if possible, be settled by agreement'. Members of the 1922 Committee did not necessarily agree that votes for all adult women were a good thing; but if they approached the prospect without rancour, it was also without enthusiasm. Mr Rentoul, who opened a discussion in February 1927, put the choice lucidly. It would be generally agreed, he suggested, that women must now have the vote on the same conditions as men, but there remained different categories of opinion which he summed up as follows :

(a) Those who would make 25 the age for both men and women;
(b) Those who thought it inevitable that 21 should be the age for both, but that it would be disastrous;
(c) Those who thought 21 inevitable, but did not fear the result.

Only one member present volunteered for the second category. The majority accepted the principle of equality of the sexes; a few even predicted that the Party might gain from the change by encouraging more women candidates. When another round of discussion took place in April, Mr Annesley Somerville, the former Eton schoolmaster who had been a founder-member of the Executive, opened by recommending 25 as the age for both men and women, and this drew a degree of support. But there was much talk about the impossibility of putting the clock back, and it was at length conceded that the best course was to submit with a good grace, since it was evident that the Government was already committed, though no one knew precisely to what, Colonel Gretton alone was left to say 'We have been stampeded!'

In March 1928, the imminent passage of the Franchise Bill caused a flurry among Members about the effect the increased electorate might have on election expenses. No less than 27 members spoke in a 1922 Committee meeting lasting only an hour. As many Members had to find their own expenses, there was a strong interest in strict limitation. Some urged that the allowance of 5d per voter should be reduced as far as boroughs were concerned; some were in favour of a decrease in the allowance for rural constituencies. There was unanimous opposition to a second free post, and a limitation on the use of posters and advertising was also suggested. On 17 April, nearly a hundred Members attended a special meeting of the 1922 called at the request of the Deputy Chairman of the Party Organisation (Lord Stanley) 'in order that certain information concerning the allowance for election expenses under the Franchise Bill might be communicated'. Despite a strong reminder that the information was confidential, and that nothing should be given to the press, full reports appeared in the newspapers the next day. This led directly to the temporary measure of issuing an agreed statement to the press, drafted by the Executive, after all meetings of the 1922 Committee 'of more than usual importance', and a warning circular was sent to all Conservative back-benchers:

CONFIDENTIAL   VERY IMPORTANT

7 June 1928

CONSERVATIVE PRIVATE MEMBERS (1922) COMMITTEE

In order that discussion at the weekly meetings of the Committee may continue to be full and frank, and that

Members may not hesitate to express for the benefit of the Committee any views that they may hold on matters of current importance, it is obviously essential that our proceedings should continue to be regarded by all Members as *strictly private and confidential*, and that no unauthorised information whatsoever should be furnished for publication to anyone outside the Committee, either as to the subject matter or as to the views expressed thereon.

During the six years that the Committee has now been in existence, it may be claimed that the occasions on which there has been any 'leakage' of information have been remarkably few, having regard to the importance and public interest of the matters from time to time under consideration, and that the privacy of our meetings has, on the whole, been well maintained.

It would be highly regrettable if this principle were to be departed from, as it would impair most seriously the admitted usefulness and influence of the Committee, both as a means of ascertaining and representing the rank and file opinion and as a 'clearing house' for information on matters of common importance to Members of our Party.

May I, therefore, venture to appeal for the close co-operation and assistance of all Members in this particular matter?

GERVAIS RENTOUL

Relations with the national press were not on the terms of familiarity which the media of today demand. Politicians were more remote, and the press less aggressive. Even so, the conviction at Westminster that it was almost always best to keep the press at a distance was very strong.

Broadcasting as a means of taking Westminster to the people was similarly suspect. In 1926, Major Harvey had ventured to speculate on the possibility of broadcasting debates in the House of Commons; not only did the Committee resolve that the proposal was 'most undesirable', but the Chairman was asked to convey that opinion to the Prime Minister. Broadcasting was of particular importance to the blind, and in 1927 Captain Ian Fraser, a future Governor of the BBC, who had lost his sight in the war, went so far as to suggest that if the last two speeches in important debates were occasionally to be broadcast, this might provide a useful corrective when press reporting was felt to be unfair. But here again, the Committee was 'overwhelmingly opposed'.

In 1928, a more querulous note could be detected in the Committee's records, as attention turned to the next election, which could not be postponed beyond 1929. The attendance of Members in the House began to fall away, and the Prime Minister sent a letter to all Conservative Members:

> The loyalty and solidarity of our Party has been for more than four years the admiration of our friends and despair of our opponents. But the approach of a General Election is having its effect. We all of us naturally feel the call of constituencies, and after so long a period of strain and stress, a certain slackening of effort is noticeable in the House during the long debates on the Local Government Acts.
>
> It does the Party harm if the idea gets abroad that attendance is falling off and majorities in divisions are wasting ...
> So I beg everyone to make a special effort ...

When it came to the Budget in April, the Committee was roused to great indignation by the obviously unpopular tax on kerosene oil, and adopted the following Resolution:

> That a deputation be appointed to interview the Chief Whip and that the strongest representations be made to him that the proposed tax on kerosene oil for domestic lighting and cooking is having the worst possible economic and political effect throughout the country.

As the Election grew closer, there was much discussion of the vast unsolved problem of unemployment; of Local Government discontents arising from the Rating and Valuation Act; of educational policy and the respective claims of Church of England and Roman Catholic schools; and of the misrepresentation of the Shop Hours Act which had alarmed the traditionally Tory shopkeeper. Before the Members dispersed to their battle grounds, however, the Committee was able to offer congratulations to the Chairman, Mr Rentoul and Vice-Chairman, Major Vaughan Morgan, on their Knighthoods. Both had served the Committee without a break since it began.

It had been expected that the Government would ask for the Dissolution as soon as the new electoral register came into force on 1 May, 1929. Election Day was set for 30 May. The fact that there were nearly a million and a half unemployed was to be the main burden of Labour and Liberal attacks. The Conservatives were unable to move away from the defensive. In the Liberal camp Lloyd George seemed to have regained, for a time, his old vigour and he put forward a detailed set of proposals to cure unemployment. The Labour Party, in fact, seemed to benefit most from Lloyd George's attack on the Conservatives' record and the Labour Party also seemed to have considerable success with the new voters. The result marked a substantial rejection of Conservative efforts: Labour won 287 seats, Conservatives 261, and Liberals 59 seats. Once again a minority Labour Administration had been returned at Westminster.

The Committee's first task on the resumption of Parliament in July, was to re-elect its Executive (Oliver Stanley was one of those chosen). Under Sir Gervais Rentoul's chairmanship the idea of an inquest was discouraged. Thus, Colonel Grant Morden's proposal to appoint a sub-committee to investigate the election result in conjunction with Central Office did not find a seconder.

But this happy state of harmony did not last for long. During the summer of 1929 there was considerable criticism of Stanley Baldwin's passive role. Once more the main bone of contention was tariff reform. In the autumn of 1929, Lord Beaverbrook and Lord Rothemere, the proprietors of the *Daily Express* and the *Daily Mail*, had increasingly committed their newspapers to a strident Empire Free Trade campaign. This, of course, meant that there would be duties to pay on foreign food from outside the Empire. The free-traders in the party, with Winston Churchill at their head, pointed out that the extension of the franchise to all adult women had increased the proportion of the electorate who were primarily interested in the cost of living.

At times Lord Beaverbrook and Stanley Baldwin seemed to be saying much the same thing about the desirability of developing Empire trade and markets, but more often they seemed to be opposed.

A 1922 Committee minute on 4 November noted that, in the course of a discussion on the political situation, 'the chief

subjects dealt with were the wisdom or otherwise of the invitation of the Imperial Affairs Group to Lord Beaverbrook to
address them on Empire Free Trade'. Apparently the balance
of opinion was in favour of the invitation.

On 4 March, 1930, Baldwin tried to resolve the dispute by
announcing at a meeting of party leaders at the Hotel Cecil
that the next Conservative Government would hold a referendum on any Empire Trade agreement that involved food taxes
– for the time being this move pleased Lord Beaverbrook, but
the split reopened.

The main battles in this war were fought in the Shadow
Cabinet, in the columns of the press, and in the constituencies;
but the 1922 Committee itself was not a forum in which the
issue of Empire Free Trade was often discussed. During the
summer of 1930, however, the controversy was raised indirectly
on a number of occasions.

On 26 May, for instance, Major Kindersley 'raised the question
of the desirability of conveying to the Leader of the Party the
view that in the event of his agreeing to form a government' (in
the case of a defeat of the Socialists) 'the re-formation of the
old Cabinet would not be acceptable'. On 2 June there was a
discussion on the Chairmanship of the Party and its duties,
(Mr J. C. Davidson, at the centre of the storm since 1929, had
just resigned, soon to be succeeded by Neville Chamberlain):
here the general feeling of the Committee was that the
Party Chairman should be appointed by the Leader as hereto-
fore.

On 17 June, Lord Beaverbrook wrote a public letter announcing that Empire Crusader candidates would be put up in every
constituency where the Conservative Member or candidate did
not support Empire Free Trade. This was an open declaration
of war.

On 23 June, Sir Neville Sandeman raised in the Committee
'the question of the attempt at dictation of the Party's policy
by sections of the press.'

To answer Lord Beaverbrook's challenge, Stanley Baldwin
called a special meeting at Caxton Hall on 24 June. Peers were
not invited. As Stanley Baldwin explained to Lord Salisbury –
'My idea has been to call together those who are actively engaged
in the constituencies as members or candidates and not to

summon a Party Meeting in the accepted sense of the term'. In fact Stanley Baldwin's counter-attack on the press lords was a triumphant success.

By 30 June, the Committee was coolly debating the merits of a proposed Central Office travel bureau, and making an appeal to members to support a performance of *Comus* at Ashridge, a large country house near London which had recently been given to the Conservative Party for use as a residential educational centre. After these domestic details had been disposed of, the Committee turned to a circular signed by Sir Henry Page-Croft suggesting the formation of a House of Commons group supporting Empire Economic Union.

The argument continued through the summer recess with notable Empire Free Trade interventions in the North Norfolk and Bromley by-elections.

At the beginning of October, Stanley Baldwin and most of the Shadow Cabinet accepted with enthusiasm a Canadian suggestion that there should be a 10% preferential increase on all duties levied on goods from outside the Empire. This was not good enough for Lord Beaverbrook, who was strongly backing an Empire Crusader candidate at the South Paddington by-election. Stanley Baldwin now decided to address a full party meeting – which included Peers receiving the Conservative Whip. The date chosen was 30 October, polling day in the Paddington South by-election. The lesson of the Newport by-election in 1922 had been learned. Stanley Baldwin was wise enough not to risk letting a shattering by-election defeat sour the tone of his own meeting. As he entered Caxton Hall, he turned to the press and announced melodramatically – 'photograph me now, gentlemen, it may be the last time you see me.' It was not. Stanley Baldwin won a vote of confidence by the sweeping margin of 462 to 116 – the party lost the by-election to Lord Beaverbrook's candidate, but Stanley Baldwin's personal ascendancy had been confirmed.

The 1922 Committee, meeting on 24 November to discuss the feeling in the constituencies concerning the activities of Lords Beaverbrook and Rothemere, recorded 'the general impression that the feeling in favour of these noble Lords and their agitation was dying, and that the Party was rallying towards unity'.

Empire Free Trade was not by any count the only Imperial or foreign issue discussed by the 1922 Committee; but up until 1930 domestic issues had far outweighed foreign affairs and defence on the Committee's normal agenda. This was partly because such matters tended to be the preserve of the specialists in the Party Foreign Affairs and Defence Committees. 1930, however, saw a distinct upward curve in the Committee's interest in foreign affairs. It could hardly be otherwise. The Fascist recoil from Communist revolution was increasingly making itself felt in Western Europe, while on the wider international stage, the mass propaganda for disarmament engaged strongly partisan feelings. In areas of entrenched British influence and specific responsibility, such as India, Palestine, and the Middle East, new forces were demanding new deals. During the period March to July 1930, the Committee heard, among others, Lord Lloyd (recently High Commissioner in Cairo) on the new treaty with Egypt, and first-hand reports on the situation in Palestine by Sir Archibald Boyd-Carpenter, closely followed by Dr Chaim Weizmann, head of the Jewish Agency. Lord Bridgeman, a former First Lord of the Admiralty, spoke on the Naval Treaty agreed in April with the United States and Japan, and Lord Stanley addressed the Committee on his visit to India where Gandhi had just been arrested.

The conflicting views on Palestine strike an all too familiar note. Sir Archibald thought that the hostility between Arabs and Jews, originally based on the land question, was assuming a religious character. Most of the immigrants from Poland and Russia appeared unfitted for agricultural work, and consequently drifted into the towns: Arabs, meanwhile, had been expropriated from their holdings. He was strongly of the opinion that some limit should be placed on the number of immigrants allowed entry. Dr Weizmann, on the other hand, considered there was plenty of room, and Arabs who had been bought out were 'doing well' in other districts. He put the figure of immigration over the past ten years at about 100,000 – large numbers of the recent immigrants had been to agricultural schools before going on the land; it was immigrant labour that had irrigated and made fertile former malaria-infected marshland, and had also created the flourishing orange groves on the coast. As for the drift to the towns, he claimed it was no greater than in other countries, and, in any case, Arabs as well as Jews were involved.

A more immediate preoccupation was the outcome of the London Naval Conference opened by King George V in January 1930. In April it was announced that Britain, the United States and Japan had reached an agreement, though they were unable to carry France and Italy with them. At a meeting of the 1922 Committee in May, after a discussion led by Admiral Beamish, a former Naval Assistant to the First Sea Lord who had commanded HMS *Invincible* at the battle of the Falkland Islands, it was decided unanimously to urge the case for a strong Party protest against the proposed Treaty in the debate on 15 May. Before that, Lord Bridgeman was again invited by the Committee to give them his opinion. He suggested it would be wiser to concentrate in the debate on pressing the Government to state the views of the Sea Lords on the proposed limitations (cruisers down to 30, for example, where the previous Conservative Government had thought that 70 should be the lowest figure) and plans for replacement; it could then be seen whether to proceed to a vote of censure. Though the feeling of the Committee still favoured outright condemnation, it was agreed to follow Lord Bridgeman's line, but to press the Leader to put down a direct censure motion on a subsequent day. After the debate, the Committee met again and adopted a resolution – after a vote – to appoint a deputation consisting of Sir Gervais Rentoul, Colonel Gretton, Admiral Beamish, Commander Southby, Lord Erskine, Major Rose and Mr A. A. Somerville to see Mr Baldwin and argue the case for censure. On 26 May, the Chairman reported that, as a result of the deputation, the Leader had agreed to demand the establishment of a Select Committee 'to examine and report upon the proposals contained in the International Treaty for the Limitation and Reduction of Naval Armaments'.

Mr Baldwin was ready to take up some of the arguments of his belligerent naval supporters. There was no real party split on this issue; but there was to be no peace for the Conservative Party, it seemed, on the Imperial front in 1930. No sooner had the Empire Free Trade controversy begun to die down, than fierce controversy within the party broke out over the future of India.

The endorsement given by Baldwin to the aim of eventual

Dominion status for India, led directly to Churchill's resignation from the Shadow Cabinet in January 1931. The split became complete in the debate in the House of Commons on 26 January, precipitating a leadership crisis scarcely less serious than the one only recently surmounted on Empire Free Trade. Once again, the 1922 Committee did not play a partisan role in the affair. That fell to the India Committee where Churchill's supporters had great influence; indeed, it seems that the India Group tended to draw off members normally attending the 1922 when the time of their respective meetings clashed. The 1922 Committee did its best, however, to be informed of more than one view. In the winter of 1930-31 it had heard experts on the legal arguments for and against constitutional reform, the special interests of the Indian princes, and the opinion of British businessmen. In February 1931, the Committee held two full-scale discussions on Indian policy and the outcome of the Round Table Conference, in the first of which Churchill took part. Yet by March it was evident to the Conservative rank-and-file, in the country as well as the Party in the House, that the attempt to shake Baldwin on the fundamental question of Indian self-government had failed.

The Committee's attention was directed, in the period up to July 1931, primarily to India, but Sir Rennell Rodd who had played an active and recent part as Ambassador in Rome was able to give members a personal assessment of Fascism in action. The Committee also heard the views of 'a deputation of gentlemen from Russia', on the current state of industry and economics in the Soviet Union including an explanation of the working of the Five Year Plan. A week later the subject was airship policy.

While the 1922 was considering the airworthiness of airships, the pound was crashing to the ground. The sterling exchange crisis marked the beginning of the end of the phase of post-war party politics which had lasted nearly a decade. The 1922 Committee met on 20 July, 1931, to hear Sir Edward Hilton Young, an expert on currency matters. The discussion was continued a week later at a joint meeting of the 1922 and the Finance Committees, addressed this time by Mr C. J. S. Mill, City Editor of *The Times*; among back-benchers taking part were Mr Robert Boothby and Mr Brendan Bracken.

This was the last meeting before the recess. On 25 August, a National Emergency Government was formed.

When Parliament resumed on 8 September, the majority of the Labour Members were ranged in virtual opposition to their leader, Ramsay Macdonald. In a political 'world turned upside down' the Tories of the 1922 discussed, at their meeting on 14 September, the question of a reduction in Members' salaries. On 21 September, Britain went off the Gold Standard. It was recognised in the 1922 Committee that a national appeal to the country was now the only realistic course, and at a committee meeting on 5 October it was generally agreed that at the coming election members should stand as 'Conservatives supporting the National Government'.

The result of the poll on 27 October, when Conservatives won 471 seats and their National Government allies won another 85, exceeded all but the wildest expectations of what might have been achieved under normal conditions. Few probably envisaged that the abnormal conditions would last much longer than a year; all were aware that there would be no lack of controversy.

In 1922, the Committee had been born out of the breakup of one coalition government. Now the Committee would have to live with another coalition. In 1929, the Committee had decided to keep '1922' in its title. It had also rejected a proposal by Sir George Hamilton to omit the word 'Private' from its title on the ground that it was desirable to include the Party leaders in the membership. Now the Committee had to consider its relations with allies in other parties as well as relations with its own Leader. Reproduced below are the minutes for 23 November, one of the first meetings of the Committee after the landslide victory:

Minutes of Meeting held on
Monday 23 November 1931 at 6 p.m. in Room 14
Present – more than 160 members.
Sir Gervais Rentoul in the Chair.

The Minutes of the last meeting was read and confirmed.

The Chairman announced that the following Officers had been elected without opposition:

Chairman — Sir Gervais Rentoul
Vice-Chairmen — Sir Kenyon Vaughan Morgan
Mr A. A. Somerville
Hon. Treasurer — Major A. J. Edmondson
Hon. Secretaries — Messrs R. H. Turton and
Reginald Clarry.

A ballot would be taken next week for the Executive Committee.

Sir Frederick Thomson attended as Whip and dealt with the work for the week.

Mr Peake made a statement with regard to a question of publicity in connexion with the India Committee.

Reports of Party Groups will be taken next week as usual when Committees have been constituted.

Earl Winterton opened a discussion on certain problems inevitably facing a Parliament with a large Government majority, referring to the experience of 1906 and 1910. There would be a danger of the dilemma of voting against the Government on one's individual conscience.

There was an interesting discussion in which the question of voting on the Statute of Westminster Bill was mentioned, and the following took part: Mr Hutchison, Sir S. Roberts, Sir M. Manningham-Buller, Mr A. A. Somerville, Mr Hales, Mr S. Samuel, Sir J. Sandeman-Allen, G. Balfour, Sir C. Oman, Mr Craven-Ellis, Mr C. Williams, and Mr Levy.

Sir F. Thomson stated there was no desire on the part of the Government to hurry the debate on the Statute of Westminster, and that more time would probably be allotted if there was a general desire.

Lord Winterton replied and was thanked for his attendance.

Adjourned at 7.20.

(signed) GERVAIS RENTOUL
(Chairman)

The problem of how to cope with a large majority, after all, is one which most political parties and most governments would be happy enough to try and deal with.

3

Smaller Battleships
(1931-33)

THE SIZE OF THE victory at the 1931 election did in fact impose
its own frustrations. Many of the back-benchers were, in
Baldwin's words, 'young, impetuous and ambitious, with no
chance of making reputations with no opposition to speak of'.
The 1922 Committee naturally felt the strain, and its diet was
made up of the domestic ingredients inseparable from the
national crisis: Sir Henry Betterton (Minister of Labour) on the
unemployment figures, and physical and educational means of
rehabilitation; Major Walter Elliot (Financial Secretary to the
Treasury) on the consolidation of Civil Service Pay; Mr Reginald
McKenna on the vices and virtues of the Gold Standard; Sir
Robert Horne and Mr Beaumont Pease on finance and currency
problems; Lord Wolmer on the 'appalling' economic muddle he
had found in the Post Office.

The laggard economy was still the central issue. In a speech
in the House on 11 June, 1932, Neville Chamberlain, the
Chancellor of the Exchequer, had declared:

> I decline altogether to accept the view (if anybody put it
> forward) that we have come to the end of the possibilities
> of reduction of our national expenditure ... But I have
> had occasion before to say to the House that if you are to
> obtain substantial reductions in national expenditure, then
> you have got to contemplate something more than a mere
> paring down, and I expressed the view that before embark-
> ing on serious changes of national policy, it is desirable
> that some hard thinking should be done. I have been
> criticised for suggesting that any hard thinking was
> necessary.

The 1922 Committee quickly picked up this gauntlet. The

Chairman proposed, at a meeting on 13 June, that a sub-committee be appointed to tackle in detail the over-riding question of how to achieve 'drastic public economy on a scale not yet contemplated'. This, Sir Gervais Rentoul contended, was the only alternative to increased taxation and needed to be faced not only by the Government, but by each individual Member. The idea of a sub-committee was supported at once by Lord Eustace Percy, who pointed out that previous economy campaigns had been hand-to-mouth, whereas the requirement now was for something more far-reaching. He saw three kinds of action open: cheese-paring by the Government (which would not meet the gap); broad decisions of Parliament (such as doing away with a whole Department); or Committee research into detail (which he believed to be the only way to get to the root of the trouble).

It was clearly Lord Eustace Percy's intervention that carried the day. He was cast in an academic rather than a partisan mould, but he was still a politician of the first rank. From 1924 to 1929, he had sat as President of the Board of Education in Stanley Baldwin's Cabinet, and he had been talked of as a future Foreign Secretary. After the defeat of 1929, he had been put in charge of the brand-new Conservative Research Department, where he had worked closely with Neville Chamberlain. By speaking at length at the beginning of the discussion, he made it plain that the Party establishment smiled on the project. It followed, after discussion, that the 1922 Committee unanimously agreed to form an Economy Sub-Committee, and Sir Gervais undertook to make the necessary arrangements.

A week after the idea had been approved in principle, Sir Gervais was able to tell the main Committee that well over a hundred Members had offered their services. It was agreed that the members of specialist groups would be chosen by the Executive. The specialist groups approved were:

(1) Local Government, including Education and Housing.
(2) Defence Services and the Central Administration.
(3) Transport and Roads.
(4) National Debt and preparation of the Estimates.
(5) Pensions, National Health and Unemployment Insurance.

At the next meeting of the full Committee the question of the

co-option of members of other parties was discussed, and it
was agreed by a large majority that the chairmen of the
various groups 'may co-opt Members of other Parties who
are supporters of the National Government, as they see
fit'.

Major Isadore Salmon, the energetic chairman of the country's
leading catering firm, J. Lyons & Co., became Chairman of the
sub-committee on the Whitehall Departments and the Defence
Services. It was suggested, irreverently, that Major Salmon had
been chosen because the Ministries and Services drank so much
tea.

Sir William Ray, a former leader of the London County
Council, was chairman of the Local Government sub-group:
Lord Eustace Percy was chairman of the Housing sub-group,
Sir Paul Latham was head of the Educational sub-committee,
and that energetic parliamentarian, Herbert Williams, led the
Public Health and Block Grants group. A member of the original
1922 Executive, Luke Thompson, was chairman of the Pensions,
Unemployment Grants and National Health Insurance group,
subjects in which he had specialised since his first election. Sir
Fergus Graham's qualifications for leading the Transport and
Roads group may not have been immediately obvious; but the
head of the National Debt group, Irving Albery, was an acknowledged expert on financial matters.

Apart from Sir Gervais and the eight sub-committee chairmen,
71 Members took part in the operation, including three women
– the Duchess of Atholl, Miss Thelma Cazalet and Mrs Shaw –
as well as five future Deputy Speakers.

The House rose for the summer recess on 16 July, but it is
clear that the activities of the sub-committees were carried on
at a considerable pace. By the time the 1922 Committee resumed
its meetings on 24 October, Sir Gervais, in addition to a progress
report, 'gave particulars regarding the publication of the Economy
Report and its presentation to the Chancellor of the Exchequer'.
On 7 November, 'The Chairman read a letter from Sir John
Ganzoni regarding the publication of the Economy Report. After
a long discussion, in which many Members took part, it was
decided to leave the matter over until 14 November, when the
Chairman would be in a position to report fully on the work
of the Economy Sub-Committee.'

To quote the minutes of 14 November:

The Chairman reported on the work of the Economy Sub-Committee. He stated that the Committee had carried out its task and that the Report would be in the hands of all Members on the following Thursday, after it had been submitted to the Chancellor of the Exchequer. He read the introductory letter contained in the Report.

Lord Cranborne objected to the publication of the Report, as he thought that the whole of the back-benchers, and especially the Tory Members, would be labelled with the responsibility for it. The Report should be neither circulated nor published.

Mr Bracken seconded this suggestion.

In a general discussion many views for and against publication were expressed. The Chairman then stated, in reply to a specific query, that he had allowed discussion on the motion put forward by Lord Cranborne in the hope that a free expression of opinion might finally satisfy the Committee that the course that had been agreed upon by the Chairmen of the Sub-Committee groups was the only practical procedure. As, however, the difference of opinion seemed so acute, he felt he had no alternative but to rule the motion out of order.

Sir Gervais Rentoul has described the background of the argument:

Immense public interest had been taken throughout in the work of the Committee, and time and again assurances had been given to the Press that the Committee would have the courage of its convictions and would publish its recommendations as soon as they were completed. We hoped thereby to show to the country how urgent was the need for economy, unless we are to regard an income tax of five shillings in the pound ... as a permanent feature of our national life.

But now that the Report was ready for publication the storm arose. Some of those who had been loudest in their demand for economy suddenly became assailed with doubts and to show signs of cold feet. Especially did this apply to some of the more recently-elected members. Although it was made clear that no one was committed by the Report except those who had sponsored certain specific recommendations, and that even individual members of the Committee could not be held responsible except for that portion of the Inquiry with which they had been directly concerned, many of the younger members of the Party began to feel like the Scotsman just before the wedding ceremony that they 'had lost their enthusiasm' ... An insistent demand therefore arose that the Report should not be published, and that the recommendations should be sent privately to the Chancellor of the Exchequer without any information being given to the Press or public as to what they were about ... In the view, however, of many other members who had devoted so much work and time to the Inquiry, this pusillanimous unwillingness to accept responsibility in a period of national emergency made one almost despair of Democracy, and they entirely refused to accede to it. An alternative proposal was that the Report should be circulated privately in the first instance to the four hundred members of the '1922' Committee and not shown to anyone else. This, however, was quite impracticable, as everyone knew who had any experience of the House of Commons. A secret that is known to four hundred, or even forty members, might as well be proclaimed from the house-tops ...

I naturally consulted those of my colleagues who had served as chairmen of the various sub-committees, as well as a number of the more senior members. I found that they were unanimously of the opinion that the whole purpose of the Inquiry would be largely destroyed if there was to be no publication, and that those concerned would inevitably be accused of not having the courage of their convictions. After full consideration, it was therefore decided that our only course was 'to publish and be damned'.*

In fact by 14 November some 5,000 copies of the 134-page report had already been printed by McCorquodale & Co. at a cost of £188 5s. 0d.

* Gervais Rentoul, *Sometimes I Think*, pp. 243-4 (Hodder & Stoughton 1940).

In an introductory paragraph, the Economy Report noted, gloomily:

> Whilst the need for a drastic and far-reaching curtailment of public expenditure, both national and local, has for many years been a popular theme on the platform, in the press, and in speeches in the House of Commons, it must be admitted that until the advent of the National Government comparatively little had been done to give to such a policy any practical effect. It is one thing to evoke enthusiastic applause from a public meeting by a reference to the necessity for economy in public expenditure, but it is quite another if the speaker attempts to enter into details. As soon as he departs from the safe path of generalities he discovers that, however popular economy may be in theory, a practical policy of economy must inevitably cut across vested interests and may well cause real and undeserved hardship to many individuals. When this happens, opposition is encountered, and public sympathy is aroused in such a way that individual considerations tend to override the broad requirements of national necessity.

The Committee noted that National Government expenditure had risen from £197,492,968 in 1913-14 to £851,117,944 in 1931-32, while local authority expenditure had risen from £104,600,000 to £319,000,000 in the same period.

The Report was published on 16 November, the day that the Prince of Wales opened the Ulster Parliament's impressive new home at Stormont Castle. It was estimated that the saving if all the proposals were adopted would amount to at least £100m. a year. The proposals were listed under various headings:

HOUSING
That all housing subsidies should be abolished, but, if necessary, in order to ensure the building of working-class houses on a scale sufficient to meet the national needs, a Housing Commission should be established to discharge the functions of a 'public landlord', and a State guarantee given to loans advanced by building societies. That local authorities should revise existing tenancies, and should, where possible, sell their houses.

That tenants who are unable to pay an economic rent on the present value of the houses they occupy should normally be relieved by public assistance, and should not receive a special form of subsidy as municipal tenants. That the Rent Restrictions Acts should be repealed for the top two of the three classes of houses which had been dealt with in the report of the Inter-Departmental Committee.

EDUCATION

That many small education departments could be amalgamated. The ratio of children to teachers could be increased.

That the present average number of full-time pupils per class in secondary schools is too low and should be substantially increased. That under present circumstances 35 children per class might be regarded as the normal maximum.

That, in view of the fact that for some years fewer teachers will be required, very substantial economies should be made in the training colleges.

That the expenditure on teachers' salaries has increased to a sum beyond the capacity of the country to bear, and a review of the whole structure of the present salary scales should be immediately undertaken. Any reduction in teachers' salaries might be accompanied by a comprehensive reduction of salaries in Local Government services.

The recommendations suggested should allow of a minimum reduction of £9,000,000, and as much as £14,000,000 if all the recommendations are fully accepted.

ROADS AND TRANSPORT

That the Ministry of Transport be abolished and that the duties of controlling and administering the Road Traffic Act and selecting schemes of highway development should be entrusted to an additional Parliamentary Secretary to the Board of Trade. That the Road Fund as such, having become a liability on the national finances, should be abolished.

That the maximum gross expenditure on roads and transport should be reduced by one-third from the 1930-31 figure of £75,715,000, and should not under any circumstances exceed £50,000,000 per annum.

EXCHEQUER GRANTS
That the Local Government Act, 1929, should be amended so as to provide for a substantial cut in the grants made under it to local authorities.

DEFENCE SERVICES
That a Committee should be appointed to examine forthwith the question of Imperial Defence as a whole. That the question of reducing *personnel* of the Admiralty and the War Office should be examined; and that an investigation of the Air Ministry should be undertaken without delay.

That Sheerness Dockyard should be closed. This would result in a saving of £140,000 after the first year.

That special attention should be drawn to the question of a possible reduction in the size of battleships, whereby an important saving could be effected. That the Royal Military Academy at Woolwich should be closed down, and all cadet training carried out at the Royal Military College, Sandhurst. That the riding establishment at Woolwich be closed down. That the possibility of abolishing the Senior Officers' School be carefully investigated.

GOVERNMENT DEPARTMENTS
Government Departments and the Civil Service. That hours of work in the Civil Service should be standardized at not less than 38½ hours net per week, to bring them into line with the LCC and other public offices.

Overseas Trade. That the Department of Overseas Trade should be wound up, and that its functions should be distributed as follows:

(a) The Commercial Diplomatic Service should be amalgamated with the Consular Service and placed under the control of the Foreign Office;

(b) the work now performed by the Department of Overseas Trade in connection with trade with the Dominions and Colonies should be taken over by the Dominions Office and Colonial Office;

(c) the remaining duties of the Department of Overseas Trade, namely, The British Industries Fair, Marketing, Trade Exhibitions, etc., should be transferred to the Board of Trade.

That the Empire Marketing Fund should be liquidated at the earliest possible moment consistent with undertakings given at Ottawa. That careful consideration be given to the possibility of economies in the Foreign Office, Diplomatic, and Consular Votes respectively.

It is urged that further consideration should be given to the proposal that the telephones and telegraph be transferred to an independent Statutory Authority constituted on the lines of the Electricity Commission.

That it is impossible for the Agriculture and Fisheries Department to exercise effective supervision while the present system of grants-in-aid exists, and that it is strongly recommended that the money now provided by appropriations-in-aid should form part of the Agriculture Vote. That the Government should make an official announcement forthwith that after 1934 no sugar beet subsidy will be given.

PENSIONS

That minor economies could be effected in both the administrative and medical divisions of the Ministry of Pensions, but that in view of the present responsibilities and at the same time steadily diminishing nature of the work of the Ministry, it is not possible to make further recommendations, especially as it is anticipated that in the course of time the work of this particular Ministry will automatically cease.

That in the administration of the Unemployment Insurance, considerable savings in expenditure are possible in the regulation of Courts of Referees, training in Transfer Instructional Centres and Government Instructional Centres. That special attention should be given to the heavy increase in staff and in expenditure on administration during recent years in connexion with Unemployment Insurance.

NATIONAL DEBT

That the allotment of estate duty revenue to a separate account, reserved for purposes of debt redemption, is urgently necessary, and that the national liability for War pensions could be transferred to this separate account for debt redemption. The constantly declining liability on War pensions will provide a substantially increasing sinking fund for the national debt.

That the opportunity should be taken at a suitable moment to issue a new form of Government bonds, which might be called 'Estate Duty Bonds', which should be issued at par and carry a low rate of interest, which would accrue cumulatively, as in the case with National Savings Certificates, and be free from income tax, surtax, and all other Government taxes.

That the handling of National Savings Certificates might now be transferred to the Post Office, in the interests of economy.

In the appendix to the Report in which 'examples of extravagance' are given, it is stated that 'in one Council authority the provision of council houses has been grossly abused, the following persons being tenants of council houses: Borough architect, sanitary inspector, clerk Education Department, clerk Engineers' Department, Grade I clerk, council rent collector, two school teachers. All the above are obviously persons in receipt of salaries considerably in excess of £200 a year. A similar position exists in many other council authorities.'

The teachers objected most strongly to the proposed cuts, but despite the fact that there were two Admirals, Sueter and Taylor, two Brigadier-Generals, Nation and Spears, and no less than eight Colonels on the Economy Committee, it was the cost of the Armed Services which received the closest scrutiny.

The sub-committee recommended, inter alia, the sale of Hyde Park Barracks, the closing of the Porton Experimental Station for Chemical Warfare (because expenditure had gone up to £79,000 in 1932), and pointed out 'that large economies might result from the closing of the Royal Naval College, Dartmouth, and the entry of all cadets through the Public Schools special entry scheme'. Sandhurst and Woolwich were to be amalgamated and the course cut to one year.

The Economy Committee was of the opinion 'that one Parliamentary representative, other than the Minister, is sufficient for each of the Service Departments'.

In the Army, we consider that the establishment of Field Marshals might be reduced to one (and that for the Indian Army also to one), that the rank of General might be abolished, and that the establishment of Lieut.-Generals, Major-Generals and Colonels might be reconsidered with a view to obtaining the maximum possible reduction. Corresponding reductions in the establishments of the higher ranks of the other services might, we believe, also be made.

We are of opinion that a Second Grade Staff Officer should be sufficient to interpret the wishes of the GOC of a Division and to issue the necessary orders. A full Colonel appears to us to be unnecessary for this purpose.

We strongly recommend that officers on the active list should not be appointed Governors of Colonies, etc., but should be required to retire when accepting such posts.

In all, the Economy Committee made nearly 140 economy suggestions. At least 100 of these were likely to give offence to some section of the community.

The result of the Report was a political, a personal and even a commercial calamity. *The Times* noted that it would be a pity 'if the value of the experiment of rank-and-file unofficial enquiry were to be obscured by doubts about the authority behind the report it produced'. *The Times* believed that even if all the recommendations were not original it showed 'a sincere appreciation of the need for securing economy in the public services without reducing their efficiency'.

The *Economist* was ruder.

What appears to have happened is that a number of sub-committees were formed, whose conclusions were arrived

at with little enough co-ordination or liaison and the result
is a medley of recommendations whereof some individual
proposals merit consideration, but whose effect in the
aggregate might well appal any Conservative Member who
lacks a cast-iron seat ... A Chancellor bent on 'contraction'
would find enough material in this report to occupy his
mind for many evenings of Budget planning, but a wiser
Chancellor would reach for the waste-paper basket. Not by
such indiscriminate lopping of services is the salvation of
England to be secured.

The *Daily Express* was still ruder. Under the heading 'The
Economy Bunglers', it thundered:

The Economy Report of the Conservative back-benchers
does disservice at once to the cause of economy, which these
members have at heart, and to the Conservative Party.

It will not do for the signatories of the report to say that
each sub-committee has been working independently of the
others, and that the findings of one section are not necessarily supported by the next section, or by the rest of the
members at large.

Explanations of this kind will not calm the fears aroused
at Sheerness Dock this morning when the people there
whose livelihood depends on the work see it proposed that
the dockyard should be closed. Nor will they comfort the
teachers who find themselves recommended for a further
salary cut, or the workmen now employed on road improve-
ments who learn that the report suggests that no new major
schemes shall be put in hand until 1936.

How much better it would be for both the party and
the nation if these MPs had joined together resolutely to
proclaim a single and coherent polity, not of economy but
of expansion and development, not of cutting down wages
and expenditure, but of building up new standards and
new prosperity.

The *Daily Telegraph*, however, thought it had all been
worthwhile:

The sub-committees have swung their axes boldly and laid
them to the very roots of the large national and municipal

expenditure which they consider should be diminished. The economies already made by the Government rendered their task to that extent the more difficult, and only a profound sense of the continued urgency of further large reductions can have persuaded these Back Benchers to brave the odium which their proposals are bound to excite among the various interests affected. But they have done what has never been done before. They have presented definite and detailed suggestions in answer to the stereotyped Ministerial rejoinder, 'Generalities about reductions are useless: Produce your plan of reform' ... The Chancellor has said that he will welcome practical suggestions. He can hardly fail to find several in this Report.

But the newspaper's Political Correspondent had an ominous comment, in the same issue:

A considerable number of Conservative MPs have taken strong exception to the publication of the report today. They belong to the Conservative Private Members' Committee – the body which appointed the Economy Committee.

These members met at the House of Commons last evening to register a protest on the subject. They attended in response to an invitation issued by Sir John Sandeman-Allen, Sir John Ganzoni, the Duchess of Atholl, Miss Horsbrugh, and Viscount Cranborne.

The ground on which they object to the course adopted is that:

'The recommendations of the five sub-committees have been made public without previous submission either to the Main Economy Committee or to the Conservative Private Members' Committee.'

In the circumstances, they contend, they cannot be held to be bound by the report. If it had been presented to them for adoption, and there had been full opportunity for an expression of their views upon it, the present difficulty would not have arisen.

The outcome of the protest meeting last evening was the adoption of a resolution expressing strong dissatisfaction with the procedure which had been followed. The whole matter will be brought up for discussion at the next meeting of the Conservative Private Members' Committee.

There has been considerable criticism of the attitude taken by the Chairman of the Private Members' Committee, Sir Gervais Rentoul. At a meeting last Monday, Sir Gervais is stated to have firmly adhered to a ruling he gave that publication of the report should precede its consideration by the Committee.

It is quite possible that, as a consequence of the indignation which has been aroused there will be opposition to the re-election of Sir Gervais Rentoul as chairman of the committee in the new session which opens next week. This is a position which Sir Gervais has filled for ten years.

As one of the members of a sub-committee, William Anstruther-Gray, a future Chairman of the 1922 Committee, noted he found himself 'bitterly attacked at the 1935 Election for views which I had never held and recommendations I had never made'.

When the Committee met again on 28 November, Sir Gervais Rentoul asked Mr Somerville to take the Chair 'while he made a personal statement regarding recent events in connection with the Private Members' Economy Committee'. On 5 December, the 1922 Committee proceeded to the election of Officers, and for the first time there was a contested election for Chairmanship, between Sir Gervais and Mr W. S. Morrison.

'193 Members were present. Mr W. S. Morrison got 117 votes. Sir Gervais Rentoul received 76.' The founding father of the 1922 Committee had been deposed.

William Shepherd Morrison, MC, a 41-year-old Scottish barrister with a commanding presence, had been called to the Bar in 1923, the year that Sir Gervais had founded the Committee. He shared with Sir Gervais an affection for the theatre – his nickname 'Shakes' was a mark of his fondness for Shakespeare. As Sir Gervais noted bitterly he 'was elected partly because he was regarded as a neutral, having hardly ever attended a meeting of the Committee, or taken any part in its struggles or activities'.

After Mr Morrison had taken the Chair Members unanimously adopted a resolution saying: 'That this Committee

expresses its sincere thanks to Sir Gervais Rentoul for his outstanding services in the Chair of the 1922 Committee during
the last ten years.'

The rest of the story is largely anticlimax. At his first meeting
as Chairman, Mr Morrison reported that he had received a
resolution submitted by several Members, asking that the
Economy Report should be considered by the 1922 Committee.
The Executive had considered the matter, and thought it better
to leave the discussion over until after the Christmas recess as
it was already 12 December. It was not until 20 February that
the postponed discussion took place, with Lord Eustace Percy
outlining the Housing recommendations; a week later Sir Paul
Latham did the same for the Education recommendations, and
the meeting ended with a vote of thanks to all the Members
who had sat on the Economy sub-committee for their valuable
work.

On 16 December, Neville Chamberlain, the Chancellor of the
Exchequer, had sent a letter of condolence to Sir Gervais:

My dear Rentoul,

I am writing to say how concerned I have been at what
seemed to me the very unfair attacks recently made upon
you. I cannot help thinking that those Members concerned
must by now feel rather ashamed of themselves about the
whole matter; and I believe some of them are already
anxious to show their feeling that you may have been hardly
treated. In any case, I am quite sure that such annoyance
as may have been caused to you will only be temporary,
and that your reputation will not in any way suffer. The
work you have undertaken has been most helpful to me
personally.

Yours sincerely,
Neville Chamberlain*

But meanwhile, another economy campaign was making life
difficult for Sir Gervais. In 1928 he had retired from the Bar
to become Chairman of the British Ironfounders Association,
but now the BIA had to curtail its activities and dispense with
Sir Gervais' services. Any prospect of a Ministerial appoint-

* Quoted from Gervais Rentoul, *This is My Case*, p. 112 (Hutchinson
1944).

ment had also evaporated with the formation of a coalition and the economy controversy. On 4 January, 1934, Sir Gervais became a London stipendiary magistrate. The disappointments of his last months in Parliament did not sour his spirit. When he died in 1946, his obituary in *The Times* noted that 'a Conservative in politics may also be an advanced advocate of legal reform ... he brought to his office a wide experience of life, and a breezy and genial atmosphere usually pervaded his court. Once he was described as an excellent magistrate for the defence, a tribute to his fairness and his desire to give a prisoner every chance.'

The Report itself seems to have been a casualty of the battle which divided the 1922. In May 1933, the Committee learned that only 1,391 copies of the report had been sold at one shilling each out of the 5,000 printed. McCorquodale & Co. were still owed £150 16s. 0d. It was resolved to discharge the account in full, and the Chairman and Sir Francis Fremantle were deputed to endeavour to make arrangements for circulation of the remaining copies now held in stock by Messrs King. A last fierce spasm of activity on behalf of the Report took place at the meeting of the 1922 on 29 May, 1933. After Herbert Williams raised the question of what had happened to the Report, Sir William Ray gave 'an interesting explanation of the present situation and the lack of Government interest in the recommendations'. A number of Members joined in the subsequent discussion, after which the following Resolution was unanimously adopted:

That the Chairman be requested to ask the Chancellor of the Exchequer or his representative if he would kindly attend the Committee to inform them of the circumstances which prevented the Government from acting upon the general recommendations of the Economy Report.

1932 marked the end of the Committee's first decade, the end of a distinguished chairmanship and the beginning and end of a notable report. The Committee had grown up.

4

National Government

(1933-39)

IN THE FIRST TEN years of its existence the 1922 Committee had become a forum in which back-bench Members could discuss every conceivable issue, and in which Ministers and Shadow Ministers could put their views to a cross-section of the Parliamentary Party.

The fact that all back-benchers could, and often did, come to the Committee meant that the discussions were often disjointed and that the main arguments about the Party's policies were usually deployed at the specialist party committees where every Member present could be assumed to have an interest in and a knowledge of the subject under discussion.

Inevitably, the 1922 Committee also became a committee of last resort, where issues could be raised that didn't easily fit into a niche provided by any other committee. Thus, inevitably, trivial domestic matters appear side by side with issues of the first rank.

In the 1930s, the 1922 also provided a platform for visiting speakers outside Parliament. Under Sir Gervais Rentoul's chairmanship, discussion had usually centred upon domestic issues, and few visiting speakers had been invited. Under 'Shakes' Morrison there was a marked increase in the number of visiting speakers and a notable shift of emphasis towards foreign affairs and defence. On the continent of Europe Hitler and Mussolini were moving to disrupt the status quo.

Not that the home front was neglected. Among the domestic issues that aroused so much interest that they spread over two meetings was House of Lords reform and the 1934 Betting and Gaming Bill.

On 23 April, 1934, Sir John Gilmour, the Minister responsible for the Betting Bill, gave the Committee an explanation of its main provisions and the purpose of the legislation. He mentioned that £25 million had been contributed to the Irish Sweepstakes and that greyhound racing had increased from one track in 1926 to 220 tracks at the present time. The objects of the Bill were to eliminate certain evils and to prevent, in his phrase, 'real rascality'. For this reason the limitation of greyhound racing was thought to be desirable. With regard to lotteries, the Government did not consider that a satisfactory way of raising money for public purposes; they understood it was not wanted by the hospitals, but the Government proposed to make small lotteries legal if they fulfilled certain conditions. Though the Bill had its Second Reading on 27 June, a number of Tory Members were still dissatisfied with the greyhound racing provisions, especially the lack of a strong enough Control Board. At the 1922 Committee on 2 July, Captain North mustered substantial support for this view, and after discussion it was proposed, and agreed unanimously, that the Chairman and Colonel Buchan should represent to the Whips and the Government 'in the strongest possible terms' the necessity for a strengthened Control Board. The Chairman also undertook to raise in these consultations a suggested permissive clause for State lotteries put forward by Sir William Davison. The difficulty in deciding what was legal or illegal when running small sweepstakes and lotteries came up in the Committee after the Act was passed, several Members complaining that it was being harshly administered, and that there was need for an authoritative interpretation by the Home Secretary.

The attention paid to this subject was not just a reflection of a widespread obsession with gambling. Small lotteries play a major role in political fund-raising for all parties.

The controversy over the Economy Report was still not quite dead. On 18 March, 1935, Mr Herbert Williams once again addressed the Committee on economy in public expenditure:

> The failure to economise between 1924-29 largely lost the 1929 Election. While the Socialists were in office many pledges to enforce economy at the earliest opportunity were made by Conservative statesmen, but these pledges had never been kept. Since the first Snowden Budget public expenditure (outside provisions for payment of debt) had

risen from £427,000,000 to £511,000,000, an increase of £84,000,000. This Parliament had proved to be the most profligate in history. During even the last twelve months our expenditure had gone up by £30,000,000 and we had been more extravagant than even the Socialist LCC. He considered that something must be done to check this spend-thrift policy. Super-tax today was showing diminishing returns and there were no further reserves left to be taxed, although we might require still further money for National Defence. If we bore in mind the fall in the cost of living it became apparent that we were today spending more than had ever been spent before in a peace-time year. The time had come when the burden of taxation must be reduced at all costs.

Mr Herbert Williams thought that the Conservative Party was taking the wrong road, but in the following week Sir William Brass, one of the 1922 intake to the House of Commons, was concerned about the speed with which the motoring public was going, and opened a discussion on the new 30 mph speed limit in built-up areas:

Dealing briefly with the past history which led up to the present restrictions, Sir William concentrated on the following six points, for further consideration in relation to the enforcement of the present regulations:

1. They take the Police from their proper duties.
2. People think that 30 mph is always safe.
3. Not elastic enough – does not take into account the condition of the road.
4. Beacons, lamps, etc., all distract the driver's attention from the road.
5. Pedestrian crossings – tests for drivers – 30 mph limit – these three new suggestions are being tried out at the same time – no one will know which scheme works best.
6. 62% of fatal accidents take place under 20 mph at peak periods.

On 11 February, 1935, the Committee first came to grips with television and Major Church, director of the Baird Television Company, attended with the object of addressing

Members on Television but as only 15 Members turned up it was decided to postpone the lecture for a fortnight. On 25 February, Major Church did give his talk to an audience of 55. It does not seem to have been a success:

His address dealt mainly with his connection with the Baird Company, and the various difficulties which the BBC had placed in the way of television experiments. He considered that his Company had been placed at a disadvantage with regard to rival concerns, and that the suggested grant of £180,000 towards television development was totally inadequate.

He produced to the Committee a somewhat formidable instrument, which apparently was meant to advertise the capacity of the Baird Company, but the Committee was not honoured with an actual experiment in television. He gave the impression that the real future of television was a Baird affair.

In the following week the Minister of Pensions, Major G. C. Tryon, talked about the 'Dangers of Socialism'.

He prefaced by some general propaganda points in favour of the National Government, instancing Iron and Steel Tariffs and the stabilising of finance.

Dealing with Socialism, he stated that it would be a dangerous experiment in this country, particularly as we were a country that could only live by exports.

On the question of personnel in Industry, he made the point that a large number of leading Industrialists had risen from the ranks, and the interests of the workers themselves would be seriously jeopardised by the control of industry passing to theorists and authors of books.

In the case of the Banks, who maintained stability during the Financial Crisis of 1930/31, by virtue of knowledge and sound control, the Socialists suggest this control should be taken over by a Socialist Government, whose main qualification was their complete failure to govern during the same period.

The effect of possible Land Taxes and Socialist confis-

cation on thousands of small landowners and householders
should be pointed out.

Major Tryon's remarks on the internal threat of Socialism
provoked a lively discussion. But in fact it was the external
dangers of Fascism, Naziism and Communism that held the
Committee's attention most often.

Many members of the Committee travelled on the Continent
and gave their own impression of events. These home-grown
travelogues were supplemented by visiting experts from
industry, banking and journalism. Most of these talks struck a
pessimistic note. An exception was provided by Miss Marjorie
Graves, who had won Hackney South at the 1931 General
Election.

Miss Graves had been a member of the secretariat serving
the Paris peace talk negotiations and was later Secretary of the
Intelligence Department at the Home Office. Her hobby was
'observing birds', but she told the Committee on 22 May, 1933,
that she had observed a May Day demonstration of over one
million Berliners 'which was a most impressive occasion, giving
much food for thought in its implications'.

Miss Graves thought that 'the exertions of the Nazi organisation were being directed towards perfecting Germany and
German in the direction of nationalism, work and discipline'.

The Minutes record that 'Miss Graves paid a tribute to Herr
Hitler's obvious sincerity and his enormous capacity for
organisation'.

Miss Graves was virtually the only speaker at the Committee
who is recorded as taking a generally optimistic view of
developments in Germany.

A most characteristic view of the European scene was given
to the Committee on 4 June, 1934, by Malcolm Muggeridge
of the *Manchester Guardian* who was described in the Minutes
as 'Mr H. T. Muggeridge, who had spent some time in Russia
as a Special Correspondent of an English newspaper'.

It is recorded that Malcolm Muggeridge 'dealt generally
with Bolshevism in theory and practice, and in particular upon
its relation to personal liberty and outlook.

'He considered that the Soviet dictators were elevating
militarism and preaching war.

'On the subject of unemployment in Russia, he stated that
it was not possible to ascertain accurate figures, as all the unemployed were driven on to the countryside to fend for themselves or to starve, and he estimated that during the last winter
over ten million people had died from starvation.

'In concluding a very interesting and cleverly-worded address,
Mr Muggeridge expressed his view that he had no confidence
whatever in the sincerity of either Russia or Germany.'

A few weeks before Malcolm Muggeridge's talk, Sir Harry
McGowan, Chairman of Imperial Chemical Industries, had
'professed that Japan will one day take a hand in policing China,
and he advised that Great Britain, if she wished to secure a
share of the Chinese market, shall undertake with Japan the
task of developing China. He was alarmed at the present dearth
of British scientific advisers in China.'

There were not many visits by Ministers during this period,
but the largest meeting of the whole 1931-35 session seems to
have assembled on 14 May, 1934, to hear Jim Thomas, the
National Labour Secretary of State for the Dominions.

> With reference to the difficult situation with the Irish Free
> State, Mr Thomas expressed the view that the policy of
> yielding to pressure by past Governments had undoubtedly
> prolonged the situation, and he believed that it was abso-
> lutely essential that His Majesty's Government should now
> act firmly in the interests of peace between the two countries.
>
> Mr Thomas stated that arrangements made at Ottawa
> had been more than justified, in spite of the present very
> difficult world economic situation, and as an illustration of
> the continuance of the good relationship between the
> Dominions, he said they had already expressed their desire
> to participate in next year's celebrations of the twenty-
> fifth anniversary of His Majesty's Accession to the Throne.

With ample evidence at hand of a rapidly deteriorating international scene, the Committee turned its attention to defence.
In the opening months of 1935 three special meetings were
held. The first, on 18 February, 1935, was addressed by Professor Lindemann of Oxford, who was known to be an authoritative adviser of Mr Churchill's on the scientific aspects of
defence.

Professor Lindemann considered that Germany at her present rate of increase would, in two years, have a military air force twice as strong as Great Britain today. The production of magnesium and gas bombs was developing very rapidly. He thought that Great Britain needed a stronger air force, but the power to inflict reprisals would not, of itself, give us full security. It was necessary to discover scientific methods for the prevention of air attack, and it was the duty of the Government to set up a special committee of picked scientific and service men to consider the whole problem. This Committee should have considerable power and their experimental work should have priority over everything else at our defence departments. Under present circumstances, the advantage of the first blow struck in the war was of overwhelming importance.

Professor Lindemann and Mr Churchill had been campaigning for a non-departmental committee for many months, and had interrupted Mr Baldwin's holiday in France in September 1934 to put their proposals before him. In fact, a committee which fulfilled some, but by no means all, of Professor Lindemann's criteria was getting under way and the first serious official discussions about the development of radar took place in the week that Professor Lindemann addressed the 1922 Committee.

On 18 April, Admiral Sir Herbert Richmond spoke to the Committee on the naval aspects of defence. He contrasted the former invincibility to invasion provided by Britain's sea-power with today's vulnerability from the air. He thought that aircraft alone could defend England against invasion. For the defence of trade it was necessary to mass together sufficient ships to keep the enemy fleet within its own waters, and in this context Sir Herbert renewed the criticism of the 1930 Naval Treaty which had been so strongly expressed by Committee resolutions at the time. He recalled that Britain's traditional policy had always been to keep her battle fleet as strong as the two principal European Powers combined; yet since the war our destroyers had been reduced from 400 to about 150, and our cruisers from 130 to about 50. Sir Herbert considered that the reductions had been far too drastic, and that unless substantial additions were made, we should not be in a position to protect our trade adequately in the event of war.

Field-Marshal Lord Milne came to the Committee on 20 May. At that moment, Lord Milne considered the chief peril lay in the East; with war between Russia and Japan almost inevitable, we should be well advised to make friends with Japan for our own security. We could not protect our vast interests in China owing to lack of bases in the Far East. Hong Kong was open to attack from land and air, and in his opinion would remain unsafe 'as long as the Washington Treaty holds', while Singapore was also in a lamentable situation. India was another weak point. Should Afghanistan ever cease to exist as a buffer state against Russia, we should at once have a 1,000-mile frontier to protect. At present we had not one more battalion of infantry at our disposal to send out to India.

Turning to home defence, Lord Milne started from the premise that England could not be defended from London, so our defence must be from the Low Countries. But we had not got the force for this today. Indeed, in his view, we were 'much worse off' than in 1914. Lord Milne suggested the possibility of international agreements on the use of air forces. He hoped that at any rate there might be some definition of what was *not* a military target.

The bankers and the diplomats also had their chance to put their views to the Committee. On 1 April, 1935, Sir George Schuster, who had been President of the British Bankers Association and Chairman of the Central Association of Bankers at the beginning of the First World War, spoke on international trade:

> With reference to one of the difficult problems – instability in exchange rates – Sir George stated that however desirable it may be to link up and stabilise the dollar to the pound, such a step was not yet possible ...
>
> Sir George particularly stressed that in his view the maintenance of our trade recovery depended on the purchasing power of our Overseas customers, particularly the producers of primary products, and it was essential that we in this country should do all we could to improve prices and consumption of agricultural production Overseas.
>
> Sir George then proposed a scheme for British regulation

of wheat imports, by making provision in this country for
a large reserve stock of wheat amounting to 220,000,000
bushels.

On 24 June, Lord Rennell of Rodd, who had been British
Ambassador in Rome, added to the prevailing mood of international pessimism:

> He considered one-sided disarmament to be folly in view
> of the increased armaments throughout the world. The
> chief cause of unrest in Europe was still the Franco-German
> antagonism, but the position between Italy and Ethiopia
> was also very serious. In the long run, the League would
> probably either have to abandon Ethiopia or lose Italy. He
> deplored the press attacks, which were jeopardising Anglo-
> Italian friendship, and he pointed out that the British Fleet
> at Malta was terribly vulnerable to air attack. He con-
> sidered that German advances of friendship should be
> received with sympathy in the hope of achieving lasting
> reconciliation.

A fortnight later Lord Rennell was followed by Sir Horace
Rumbold, the British Ambassador in Berlin from 1928 to 1933.
Sir Horace did not think there was much chance of any recon-
ciliation with Germany, because of the blood-thirsty qualities
of the Nazi Government:

Sir Horace cited Hitler's 'clean-up' of the Nazi Party, when
200-300 men were shot in cold blood without trial. It was
hardly necessary to remark that overtures of friendship with
Britain should be accepted with mental reservations. Giving
character sketches of some of the leading personalities in
Germany, he described Goering and Goebels as 'pathological
cases, who were handling an under-nourished generation'.

While the 1922 Committee heard speaker after speaker calling for caution and rearmament, the mood of the electorate
seemed to be moving in the opposite direction.

On 25 October, 1933, East Fulham, a seat formerly held by
Sir Kenyon Vaughan Morgan, one of the Committee's vice-
chairmen, was captured by the Labour Party. The Labour
candidate had made disarmament the major issue of the campaign while the Conservative candidate had urged that Great

Britain's defences should be maintained. Throughout the winter of 1933 and into 1934, there were a string of sensational swings against the Government, which the commentators of the day ascribed to the latent pacifism of the British electorate. On 15 February, 1934, the by-election following the retirement of Sir Gervais Rentoul was held at Lowestoft. Once again the swing against the Government was enormous – 19.9%, and once again disarmament was thought to have been the key issue. It is not surprising that this calamity in their former Chairman's seat should concentrate the mind of the Committee.

Meanwhile, the Government was clearly shifting its ground in the face of a developing threat in Europe and the Far East. In the early 1930s Stanley Baldwin had believed with conviction, and even passion, in the need for multi-lateral disarmament. During the first years of the National Government, Stanley Baldwin continued to play a dominant role in the formulation of official defence policy in the Cabinet's Committee on Imperial Defence. In the mid-nineteen-thirties the looming failure of the International Disarmament Conference, Japan's expansion in the Far East, Italy's assault on Abyssinia and Germany's threatened rearmament, had altered the balance. The policy of the Conservative leadership was changing from disarmament to rearmament, a shift which was symbolised by the alteration in May 1935 of the title of the Ministerial Committee on Disarmament to the Committee on Defence Requirements. It is clear that a majority of the Members of the 1922 Committee favoured this change of emphasis.

In the foreign and Imperial field only one dominant issue went almost wholly undiscussed by the 1922 Committee. In 1934 and 1935 the issue of Indian Home Rule provoked much the same degree of division within the Conservative Party that entry into the European Economic Community provoked in the early 1970s. At the 1933 Party Conference, a resolution directly hostile to the White Paper on Indian constitutional reform issued by the Government in June was defeated by 737 votes to 334. In the House of Commons nearly seventy Conservative Members of Parliament, led by Winston Churchill, supported the India Defence League. At the Conservative Party Conference in 1934, the vote in favour of the Government's policy on India was carried by 540 votes to 523, a margin of 17. Members of Parliament and their constituency associations were often in sharp disagreement, but during the three years in which the Indian issue divided the party, it was rarely discussed in the 1922 Committee. On 20 March, 1933, Members attended a joint meeting with the India Committee 'during which twenty-five members addressed the Committee and expressed their views'. This did not mean that the Parliamentary Party failed to discuss this subject, but it did mean that the bitter argument was carried on in the specialist committees and not in the 1922 Committee itself.

When the House dispersed for the summer recess in 1935, there was yet no announcement of a forthcoming election, though the likelihood was strong that it would be held in the autumn.

In his eventual decision not to delay the General Election beyond November, Baldwin is said to have been influenced by the urgency of the foreign policy problems, which seemed only too likely to grow worse by postponement. Polling day was set for 14 November. During the campaign a number of those who had served on the Economy sub-committees were attacked for that document, but politically this was ancient history. The anti-Government, pro-pacifist tide so visible at the by-elections of 1933 and 1934, was dramatically reversed. The result swept the Conservatives back into power on a platform of collective security which, while it acknowledged the need for rearmament, emphasised the need for fresh efforts to breathe life into the League. After a poll of over 70%, the Conservatives held 432 seats to Labour's 154, and the Liberals' 30. There could be no doubt of the mandate.

Parliament assembled on 3 December, and a week later the 1922 Executive met to arrange the Committee's own elections. As Mr Morrison had been appointed Minister of Agriculture in the new Government, the Chairmanship was open. Four names were put forward for the post: Mr Reginald Clarry, the victor of Newport and a founder member of the Committee; Sir John Ganzoni, a barrister with a passion for lawn tennis, who had taken a leading role in the attack on the Economy Report; Sir Hugh O'Neill who had already been the Member for Mid-Antrim for seven years when the 1922 Committee was first formed, and had also been the first Speaker of Stormont; and Mr Ronald Ross, who was a barrister like Sir John, an Ulster

Unionist like Sir Hugh, and an old Etonian also like Sir Hugh.
On the first count there was a tie between Mr Clarry and Sir
Hugh O'Neill. On the second ballot, Sir Hugh was elected by
82 votes to 58. At the previous election in December 1934,
there were no contests and only 25 Members had bothered to
attend. Mr Morrison had not been an energetic innovator like
his predecessor, Sir Gervais Rentoul, but he had guided the
Committee with distinction through a difficult period of transition.

The Committee's custom of inviting the Chief Whip to
address the first full meeting at the start of a parliamentary
session, was observed in February 1936, with some 100 Members
present. After this General Election there were comparatively
few new Members, and Captain Margesson came to the point
with characteristic directness. Members were reminded of the
importance of regular attendance upon Standing Committees,
and were urged not to leave the house by 'bolt-holes' – for which
the geography of the Palace of Westminster would seem specially
designed.

At the next meeting, Miss Irene Ward, who had just been
re-elected for Wallsend-on-Tyne, opened a discussion on 'The
Problem of Retaining Precarious Seats'. Miss Ward claimed that
the work done inside and outside the House during the last
Parliament had largely broken the old allegation that the Conservatives were a 'rich man's party'. Finally, Miss Ward claimed
from the Leader and the Whips 'an occasional licence for
Members with difficult seats' to vote against the Government.
Only one of her listeners had the temerity to dispute this point.

It was a characteristically robust performance from a Member
who has intervened in the Committee's deliberations more frequently than any other single individual in the course of its
first fifty years. As one retired Whip remarked, 'I could always
tell when Irene was going to make a fuss, because she would be
wearing a new hat. At times it seemed that she had an in-
exhaustible supply of millinery.'

Meanwhile, the Executive Committee soon turned to planning
the dinner to the Prime Minister on 21 May. It was the last
occasion of its kind that Mr Baldwin would attend. Claridges,
where it was originally intended to hold the dinner, proposed a
charge of 12s 6d per head, or 1 guinea inclusive of wines (to

be chosen by the Treasurer, Major Edmondson). But, in fact, the dinner was held in the House of Commons. Besides Mr Baldwin, Captain Margesson (Chief Whip), and Captain Hacking (Party Chairman), the Committee invited their two ex-Chairmen, Mr W. S. Morrison and Sir Gervais Rentoul. In this congenial atmosphere Baldwin struck a reminiscent, even elegaic note. In his own words:

> The 1922 club gave me a dinner in the House the other night, and I think I had a great success. There were from 130-150 present, and I spoke for about three-quarters of an hour. I had just a note or two to keep me right. I said there were some who doubted whether I was a dyed-in-the-wool Tory. I told them I wore the Tory colours in my pram in the 1868 election. My father voted Whig then, but our cook was a Tory and she saw to my politics. For 94 years a Tory had represented Bewdley. I told them of my fight at Kidderminister, how I had come back from a visit to the United States as a protectionist, how we were stirred by Joseph Chamberlain's tariff campaign, how we blundered badly over the Taff Vale decision, how when the war ended, we were in a new world, but how class-conscious and revolutionary it was; how I felt that our Party was being destroyed and how I determined to do what I could to rescue it. I did not mention L.G. or Winston. Then in 1931 we conformed to the King's wish and all my colleagues agreed with me in doing so. I then touched on German re-armament and claimed that we could not have got this country to re-arm a moment earlier than we did.[*]

Mr Baldwin's reminiscences were primarily domestic, but the Committee's domestic programme during the first year of Sir Hugh O'Neill's chairmanship looks, in retrospect, somewhat inadequate. The solicitor of the Football Pool Promotions Association discussed his problems. Mr Alan Herbert recommended his Private Members Bill on Marriage Reform and 'remarked that in many countries in which divorce for desertion is legally possible, there was no evidence that morals were worse.

---

[*] Keith Middlemas and John Barnes, *Baldwin* (Weidenfeld and Nicolson 1969), p. 933.

than in this country'. A more querulous note was struck on 9 November, 1936, by Captain Gunston, who had heard a rumour that at the forthcoming Coronation Service Dowager Peeresses would get preferential allocations of seats in Westminster Abbey. He hoped that representations would be made to stop Members being 'crowded out by dowagers'. (The Chairman of the 1922 Committee was not consulted by Mr Baldwin during the abdication crisis, which was imminent.)

But under Sir Hugh O'Neill as in the days of 'Shakes' Morrison's chairmanship, foreign affairs dominated the scene. Here family interest matched the pressure of events, for Sir Hugh's son, Con, had recently entered the diplomatic service and would soon be posted to Berlin.

Major-General Sir John Davidson, who had been Chief of Operations at GHQ in France towards the end of World War I – and who had been a Member of the Committee before the 1931 election – called for 'a very careful organisation of industry in preparation for War, on the grounds that full industrial mobilisation would be required in the event of another conflict'.

Field-Marshal Sir Philip Chetwode did not see much use for the 'Air Arm' in India. He advocated the slow and gradual Indianisation of the Army, such as is at present being carried out. He did not look upon the present rate of change in this direction as being dangerous, though he regretted that the Army was not getting enough of the right class of Indian Officer.

On the following week, Sir Bernard Pares, the distinguished observer of Russian events, reported that:

Russia expects war and is afraid of German expansion. Hitler has killed the possibility of a Russo-German alliance and the tendency of Germany today is to spread eastwards. The Japanese Government is Nazi in origin, which increases the likelihood of a real German-Japanese alliance. If Germany captures the Ukraine, it means the end of Russia in Europe.

Sir Bernard pointed out that Russia's fear of Germany has led to a change in her internal policy. 1932 was a year of intense oppressive legalisation, but since then there has been a steady drift to the right, probably led by the Government. Piece-work is now encouraged, and the class qualification for entry to the Universities has been abolished. Every peasant can now own 3 cows and as many pigs and poultry as he likes. The Ballot is to be restored and the voting power of the peasants is to be increased.

Religion is not dead, and a Christmas Eve Service in Moscow is packed like an English Cup-Tie.

Sir Arnold Wilson, a Member who had a distinguished career in the Persian Gulf before entering the House, addressed the Committee twice. After a visit to Germany and Italy, he reported that Italy no longer feared oil sanctions after her attack on Abyssinia 'as she has now built up immense reserves of oil'. In Germany, he reported that 'the Nazis were not anxious to promote paganism, but they wish to bring the German church into the same position as the Church of England. Germans protest ... that they have no designs on Czechoslovakia. They wish for an outlet and mean to have Austria.'

Later in the year, Sir Arnold reported on the Middle East with particular reference to Iraq. 'The King was quite ineffective, although educated at Harrow.' 1936 marked the beginning of the Arab revolt in Palestine. Sir Arnold thought that at least as far as Iraq was concerned:

There is no real anti-Jewish feeling there; it is simply used as a stick to beat the British with and the more we give way the more we shall be kicked ... Anyway the Arabs will only bow to force.

The Marquis of Londonderry, who had fought hard for the resources to build up British air defences when serving as Secretary of State for Air before the 1935 General Election, took a relatively optimistic view after his trip to Germany following Hitler's march into the Rhineland:

He thought that the people and the Government were anxious for the friendship of Britain. There was considerable expenditure upon armaments, but the figures had to be taken with reserve. The German organization was so powerful that it could be switched into dangerous channels. Hitler appeared to want peace and the Government would favour an understanding with both Britain and France. Germany feared the possibility of encirclement, and Hitler had a genuine obsession with regard to the Bolshevist character of Russia. He would like the Colonies back but was not prepared to fight for them.

But the most contentious issue of the day was certainly sanctions against Italy. On 3 October, 1935, after months of threats, alarms, marches and counter-marches Italy had invaded Abyssinia. On 11 October, the Council of the League of Nations had set up a Committee of Eighteen to decide what action should be taken to try and halt this Italian aggression. By the end of October, largely as a result of Anthony Eden's prodding, it was decided to impose certain sanctions on Italy. There was to be an embargo on Italian imports, certain financial restrictions and a limited ban on exports to Italy, including certain strategic materials such as rubber, tin and scrap iron. These restrictions came into force on 18 November, but their effectiveness was blunted as a number of countries did not enforce them. It was soon argued that sanctions had failed, and on 24 February, 1936, Sir Arnold Wilson had reported to the Committee the view of Mussolini that 'sanctions and Mr Eden had united modern Italy'. On 25 May, a formidable attack was made on the sanctions policy by a senior diplomat, Sir Francis Lindley, who had recently retired as Ambassador in Japan, another country in conflict with the League after the assault on Manchuria:

He said he had always been against sanctions because, unless we were prepared to go to war, they must be useless. He claimed that the League should be reformed and the penal clauses abolished. He pointed out that we have neither the advantages of the old diplomacy nor of the new. In the case of the Manchurian affair, the fault was not all on one side. We should at once have told the Chinese to negotiate, which the Japanese were willing to do. This was stopped by the intervention of the League of Nations which, by butting in, destroyed the chances of settling this dispute in a sensible way by diplomacy. China, as a result, lost five provinces. Under the present covenant disputes could neither be settled by force, because force was not there, nor in a common-sense way, by negotiation. He said it had been known for a long time that Germany was heavily re-arming. We must make it clear that we were not going to be involved except for the defence of the Channel ports and our own Empire.

When the Committee met on 15 June, Mr Maurice Petherick drew attention to 'the admirable speech' made by Mr Neville Chamberlain the Chancellor of the Exchequer at a 1900 Club dinner on 10 June, 1936. He had denounced sanctions in much the same terms as Sir Francis Lindley, and had already caused much comment in Westminster since he appeared to have repudiated unilaterally the very policy his Government had initiated and still supported when the speech was made. Mr Petherick commented that the Chancellor had 'sent up a trial balloon', and that his suggestions would be welcomed by the nation as a whole. Sanctions should be buried at once and the penal clauses eliminated from the League Covenant at an early date. According to the Committee minutes:

> An animated discussion followed in which 17 members took part. The unanimous view was expressed that Sanctions had failed and should be removed. There was a general feeling that the Covenant should be revised. The Chancellor's pronouncement was approved by most speakers, although a few Members considered that his speech had been made at an inopportune moment.

Mr Baldwin, in fact, had already suffered the embarrassment of a Private Notice Question by Mr Attlee as to the meaning of the Chancellor's *ex cathedra* pronouncement, and had been forced back on the reply that Mr Chamberlain's speech was only 'a personal reflection delivered to an exclusive audience of politically educated people'. But a few days later, the Government formally announced the abandonment of the Sanctions policy. These followed an Opposition motion of censure on 23 June. Harold Macmillan and one other Conservative Member voted against the Government.

The Committee had not been much reassured by its only Ministerial speaker of the year, Sir Thomas Inskip, who had been translated to the new post of Minister for the Coordination of Defence from his old post as Solicitor General, where he had won a reputation for competence and caution.

In discussing the question of supply he said that his duties were, so to speak, to oil the wheels. The Departments engaged found it difficult to organize industry so as to produce all that is required at once. He hoped, however, that it would be possible to complete the programme within the period laid down of three to five years. He remarked that strategy was now more difficult than ever owing to the impossibility of foreseeing the circumstances under which a war might break out or what countries would be involved. He was, he said, daily more impressed by the close relation of foreign policy and defence. He considered that, as a result of scientific research, the submarine menace has been reduced to manageable proportions. He was most hopeful about the results of research in relation to the air menace. The question of the advisability of setting up a Ministry of Supply was constantly under review.

Sir Thomas Inskip had been listened to by 100 Members. Winston Churchill was listened to by 150 Members, when he addressed the Committee on 7 December 1936, two days before the abdication of King Edward VIII. Although many commentators were arguing that Mr Churchill's influence had been reduced by his support for the King, he attracted the largest audience at any meeting of the 1922 Committee in 1936. His message was clear:

Mr Churchill claimed that we started re-armament two years later than we should have, and that there must be a dangerous hiatus until full fruition is reached. The danger point will be, he said, when German re-armament has been achieved and we are still not fully prepared. He declared that in the circumstances it is wiser in public to concentrate now on the appearance of strength rather than insisting too much on our weaknesses. He laid weight on the power of the Navy and the improvement since last year's crisis in the Mediterranean. He mentioned our weakness in face of Japan in Far Eastern waters and laid stress in particular on the importance of the base at Singapore. He said the Navy should have control of all aeroplanes used from ships, but that otherwise, in the main, the War Cabinet should act through the Air Force and the Air Ministry in the event of war.

He said we should accept the report of the Committee

on Capital Ships, and does not believe they are useless in face of an air attack. Concerning the Army, he advocated an increase in mechanization and mobile power. He said that, if it were not for the air, we should not have so much cause to worry, but as the air is now a fighting element we were in a most vulnerable position. He believed that the Germans will, by 1 January, have about 1,800 first line machines, plus 200 Lufthansa machines convertible into bombers. In addition, they have, he thought, about 1,500 in reserve and some 450 training machines which, in the event of a short war, could be used for fighting. He said that, by 1 January, we should have 80 squadrons for home defence, some of them skeletons. But even this only means 960 machines, and this is half the German strength. He also feared that as we are obliged to use old models in order to get rapidly up to strength, our machines were inferior to the newest type of German ones. With the French, he said, we should in time of war be formidable, but he did not think that now both countries together were the equal of the Germans. Finally, he said the defences of London were deplorably weak, and must be put in order.

The Committee's Chairman, Sir Hugh O'Neill, had been a member of a deputation, led by Churchill and Sir Austen Chamberlain, which had called upon Mr Baldwin in his room at the House on 28 July, 1936. Their basic theme, developed on two successive days, was priority for rearmament and the need to recover lost ground; but throughout 1936 the Committee's records give the impression that Members were well-informed and concerned spectators rather than active participants in an attempt to resolve a deepening crisis.

1937 opened with no change in the office-holders of the Committee and its Executive. All had been re-elected without a contest, but before the year ended there was an alteration in the rules. It was agreed that the three senior members of the Executive should retire each year in rotation, and not be eligible for re-election for the duration of the session. The year's subscription was again kept to five shillings.

In January, a Government decision to build an aircraft factory in the rural area of White Waltham brought into play at least three of the Committee's main interests – rearmament, work for the depressed areas and the preservation of rural amenities. The central objection, strongly expressed by Sir Reginald Clarry, was that the Government proposed not only to destroy amenities by placing the factory in an agricultural area and wasting money building a new town, but also that there were many 'distressed areas' suitable for, and in urgent need of, the work such a factory would provide. Sir Ronald Ross protested that Northern Ireland, which had proportionately larger unemployment than in the rest of the United Kingdom, had been left out of the rearmament programme, and there was no excuse for the Air Ministry. The Government evidently had second thoughts, and it was announced the next day that an alternative site was being sought in industrial Lancashire. The factory was eventually sited on the outskirts of Liverpool.

A landmark of sorts was reached on 22 February, 1937, when the Committee held its first full discussion on left-wing bias in the BBC.

It was argued that 'broadcasts of a subversive character were given to the schools which aimed at showing that conditions were better in Russia than at home'. It was also argued that the BBC's reporting of the Spanish Civil War was 'very unfair'. This was the first, and almost the last, reference to the Spanish Civil War in the Committee's records.

There was a widely-supported proposal that scripts of BBC broadcasts should be deposited in the Library of the House of Commons so that Members could keep themselves informed on points of controversy. The Chairman agreed to see the Postmaster-General, Major Tryon, and also to try and get him to address the Committee at an early date and to bring Sir John Reith with him. Sir John had had an enthusiastic reception when he last attended a meeting of the Committee in March 1934.

Before the proposed meeting took place Sir Alfred Knox put a Question to the Postmaster-General, asking whether there was 'any practical difficulty in furnishing to the House of Commons Library daily verbatim reports of broadcasts' so as to check complaints of constituents. Major Tryon replied that the request could not be regarded as reasonable in view of the volume of material involved. Sir Alfred was not pleased, and raised the matter on the Adjournment, but with no further success. On 8 March, Sir Hugh O'Neill himself renewed the attack with a Question little different from that originally put by Sir Alfred Knox, though this time he received a softer answer. The BBC, said Major Tryon, would be willing to furnish any Member, on request in writing, with a copy of any particular script. This compromise has been in operation ever since.

On 15 March, Major Tryon and Sir John Reith came to the Committee as had been requested. Sir John held the floor in the opening stages of discussion, saying he realised there was room for improvement in the BBC's relations with Parliament, and he wished to obtain the sympathy and support of the House. He did not accept that the BBC was insensitive to criticism; rather, he felt, the House failed to recognise the BBC's difficulties in steering a course between over-caution and the abuse of its responsibility to exercise self-control. Major Tryon, for his part, insisted that the House would be wrong to ask the Government to control the BBC. He was certain that the present system of keeping it an independent Corporation was far the safest.

In the first months of 1937 there was rather more contact with Ministers. The 1922 Committee heard Mr Duff Cooper and Lord Swinton (respectively War Minister and Air Minister) report fairly satisfactory progress in recruiting for the Army and Air Force, though in both services the provision of up-to-date equipment was not yet up to schedule. The first plans for air raid precautions were outlined by Mr Geoffrey Lloyd (Under-Secretary at the Home Office) at a committee meeting early in March. The work of organising ARP had been started by a secret sub-committee of the Committee of Imperial Defence. This later handed over to a Home Office Department which issued its first circular to local authorities in the summer of 1935. Mr Lloyd reported very considerable headway since then by way of Local Authority schemes for first aid, rescue parties and decontamination squads, the free supply of respirators for the civilian population and the rapid training of the medical profession in anti-gas treatment.

The rather strained climate of opinion encouraged discussion in the Committee of such phenomena as 'mysterious fires' and rumours of sabotage in munition factories, the activities of the

Left Book Club, and the misrepresentation practised by some of the 'Peace Campaigns'.

The delicate matter of revision of Ministers' salaries, which had seemed relegated to indefinite postponement in 1928, came to the fore in April 1937, when Mr Baldwin introduced the Ministers of the Crown Bill in one of his last speeches as Prime Minister.

This Bill (which, for the first time, gave a salary to the Leader of the Opposition as well as increases for Cabinet Ministers, with proportionate increases on the lower rungs of the ministerial ladder), gave impetus to the related question of Members' pay, in which the Labour Party had already declared their interest. The initiative for a discussion in the 1922 Committee came from Mr Edward Keeling on 19 April, a few days after Mr Baldwin had undertaken to consult the Opposition leaders as to the position – and hardships – of MPs. The reaction of Conservative back-benchers was mixed. Mr Keeling thought there was a good case for an increase in the existing rate of £400 a year 'owing to the rise in the cost of living since 1911, the growth of the electorate, and the fact that autumn sessions had become common form'. He considered the real test to be what was now the minimum salary upon which a Member could live, and he regarded £600 a year as a not unreasonable figure. Major Mills, supporting this argument, pointed out that the original payment had not, in fact, produced a worse type of Member. But Mr Wise was just as strongly opposed to an increase, claiming that constituency expenses now were less than pre-war, and that Members' salaries were never meant to do more than cover personal expenditure: 'If salaries were to be paid for services rendered, he thought he was worth at least £2,000 a year.' Miss Florence Horsburgh made the astringent comment, that any increase in salaries might simply encourage constituencies to contribute less to organisation and election expenses. No vote was taken in the Committee, but the following conclusions were put on record:

That a considerable body of Members regarded any increase at the present time to be inopportune and electorally dangerous, but many Members favoured the idea of some sort of pensions scheme. The Chairman undertook to convey the feeling of the meeting to the proper quarter.

However, an increase to £600 a year was recommended by the Government, and approved by the House of Commons in June, with only 17 dissentients. As Mr Baldwin declared: 'I think, looking at the whole Continent of Europe, that the more the basis of our liberty and our Constitution is broadened, the better for our country. Would anyone who remembers the old days here go back to them and give up what we have gained? This Chamber, the most famous Chamber in democratic government in the world, is now open to all and once you admit that everybody has a right to be elected to this House if he can, you cannot logically create or have a financial bar.'

Of the 17 who voted against the increase 14 were Conservatives, including Mr A. A. Somerville, Joint Vice-Chairman of the 1922. The pensions question was to provide further discussion in the Committee a year later.

The announcement on Members' salary was to be Mr Baldwin's last noteworthy appearance in the House as Prime Minister. He had been leader of the Conservative Party ever since the formation of the 1922 Committee.

After Neville Chamberlain had succeeded Mr Baldwin as Prime Minister, the Committee's interests continued to see-saw between purely internal Party matters and international issues. At the meeting on 21 June, 1937, for example, Mr Herbert Williams raised the question of the proposed alteration in the National Union rules which laid down that no candidate adopted by a local Association would be accepted as official unless endorsed by Central Office. To this the Committee objected, and Sir Hugh O'Neill was empowered so to inform the Party Chairman. Sir Arnold Wilson then followed with a critical assessment of current decline in Army recruiting. On the present form he forecast a 50,000 deficiency in twelve months' time and the number of reservists considerably less than in 1914. Sir Hugh O'Neill was requested to see the new War Minister, Mr Hore-Belisha, with the result that the Minister came to the Committee in July for a full discussion of recruiting problems:

With reference to pay, he mentioned that the basic pay was the same for the three services and therefore it was difficult

to raise it, but he thought a more hopeful line of approach
was to give increased special allowances, such as trades-
men's allowances, etc. He discussed various internal reasons
for the unpopularity of the army. He also said that he intended to try and raise the tax status of the territorial army
and to begin by improving the status of the Director-
General of the Territorial Army, giving him complete
control over it.

Exactly one year after Mr Churchill had addressed the Committee, Captain Liddell Hart, the military expert who was a
close adviser of Mr Hore-Belisha, the Secretary of State for War,
gave the Committee his view of the military threat:

He thought the air weapon was in favour of the defence.
He said he considered that, other things being equal, the
attackers required a three-to-one preponderance in order to
be successful.

On the strategical question he declared that until the
'nineties of the last century, German strategists were opposed
to a Western offensive, and that in 1914 it was due to political considerations that Germany struck that way. It was
only owing to a French error that she was almost successful.
He said it would be more difficult now owing to the strength
of the Maginot line. He believed that any German offensive
westwards was unlikely.

On the East, he thought it possible that she might strike
at Czechoslovakia, but it was a mistake to underestimate
the Czech army. Poland's attitude appeared to be doubtful,
and it would be difficult to get up Russian and Roumanian
help, except by air.

He thought that the Italians were unlikely to succeed in
an attack against France, but that they could be dangerous
in North Africa. He was also doubtful about the Spanish
attitude, and feared the possibility of a hostile Spain making
bases available for the enemy.

He thought we should be unwise to send more than a
very small force, and that a mechanized one, on to the
Continent, and that our force would be better employed in
the Empire where we are heavily under-insured.

The year 1938 began and continued on a low note. In February, following Anthony Eden's resignation, a meeting on Palestine to be addressed by Norman Bentwich had to be postponed because most members had gone to listen to the foreign affairs debate. Among those who abstained from voting with the Government in the Division, were a fair number of past and present Members of the Executive, including Mr Robin Turton, Mr Emrys Evans, Sir Joseph Nall, and Major Hills. A few weeks later, the Minister of Labour's comments on the cost of living index also had to be postponed because Members had flocked to a defence debate. Throughout the spring and summer of 1938, attendance often dropped below fifty and never rose above a hundred. While the temperature of the national debate on defence increased markedly outside the Committee, it showed an equally noticeable decline inside.

On domestic issues, discussions ranged from the cost of living to the Carlisle experiment in state-owned pubs; and from fuel policy to the effect of Entertainments Duty on the living theatre.

In May 1938, a considerable shock was caused by the resignation of Lord Swinton, Air Minister since 1935, whose presence in the Upper House prevented him from conducting his own defence against charges, made in a Commons debate, of insufficient progress in air rearmament. His successor, Sir Kingsley Wood, addressed the Committee in July; and after paying tribute to Lord Swinton's work, went on to emphasise the significant part now being played by mass-production methods in setting new targets in aircraft production. Among the tycoons involved in developing these methods, he mentioned Lord Nuffield, who had been given a 'free hand' in his new works, the number of types being reduced to a minimum with the aim of achieving maximum standardization. Sir Kingsley also spoke of the possibility of setting up aircraft works in Canada, and asked for the help of Members in recruiting 31,000 men.

The House rose, as usual, at the end of July, having heard Mr Chamberlain declare, on the eve of their departure to the constituencies, that he now saw signs of a relaxation of tension on the Continent as a whole.

The emergency recall of Parliament on 28 September, the eleventh-hour gesture from Hitler and Chamberlain's response, the mass surge of relief and then the recoil from the supposed settlement at Munich, all took place without a meeting of the 1922 Committee.

In fact, the 1922 Committee did not resume its regular meetings until the new parliamentary session in November. Elections for the ensuing year took place as usual, with no change of Chairman or Officers. But when the Committee did meet, there was a rather greater sense of urgency. On 14 November, for example, the first item of business after the elections was an application from the newly-formed ARP group for affiliation with the Committee. The question of the proposed loan to Czechoslovakia was then raised by Sir Walter Smiles, 'who thought the money might be better spent at home, or a lesser sum given outright'. Next, Sir Stanley Reed 'expressed doubts on the wisdom of our guaranteeing the new Czech frontiers', while Mr Henry Strauss introduced the colonial question 'mentioning a strong rumour current in France about the cession of Nigeria'. After a number of Members had discussed re-armament and manpower, Mr Herbert Williams and Mr Maurice Petherick spoke against the establishment of a National Register.

The question of a National Register was the most important subject discussed by the Committee in the immediate post-Munich period. The 1922 Committee had been interested in the possibility since Sir Edward Grigg had addressed the Committee on 16 May, when he argued:

Speeding up re-armament was not enough, organisation of the nation was essential. 'Key-men' had been recruited into the Anti-aircraft Units and would not be available when required. Three things were necessary for efficiency: (1) Compulsory National Registration: (2) Concentration on the organisation for defence of vital spots: (3) Setting up of Air Defence Authorities for important areas. The moral effect of such action on Germany would be tremendous.

When the Executive met shortly before the new Session, it was decided that Sir Hugh O'Neill and some of his colleagues should see the Chief Whip to request 'that if mention was made in the King's Speech of a National Register, the Register should not be voluntary'. It was widely recognised that compulsory registration might well have to be followed by compulsory service.

On 1 December, Sir John Anderson, now Lord Privy Seal, announced that the Government proposed to draw up a National Voluntary Register. He recalled that there had been much speculation during the last few months about a compulsory Register, but the Government had come to the conclusion this was neither necessary nor desirable; the need would best be met by a voluntary Register 'combined with measures to ensure that all who wish to serve shall have the means of knowing how that service can best be utilised'. A handbook would be prepared, setting out particulars of the types of men and women most suitable. At this stage, the Government did not consider any legislation was needed.

When the House reassembled after Christmas, the Committee's opening discussion was devoted to the question of the evacuation of school-children and others from danger areas. Members who had experience in their constituencies of the experimental evacuation at the time of Munich, were asked foɪ their views. In February 1939, Sir Herbert Emerson, the League of Nations High Commissioner for Refugees, gave the Committee an account of the work being done on another sort of evacuation – of Jewish refugees from Germany. Sir Herbert said the problem now was to evacuate in five years 150,000 wage-earners, to be followed by 250,000 dependants, as well as to aid as far as possible other non-Jewish and political refugees. Some 200,000 German Jews had been dealt with since 1935, mostly by infiltration into countries of temporary refuge. The problem of long-term settlement was only now being seriously tackled. 'As regards possibilities in British Guiana, Northern Rhodesia and San Domingo, it was not possible to speak till expert commissions had reported.'

On 6 February, preliminary arrangements were discussed for a dinner to the Prime Minister: but before it took place, virtually all that remained of the Munich agreement had collapsed with Hitler's march into Czechoslovakia.

The shock effect of Czechoslovakia's betrayal was evident both in the urgency of discussion as to the introduction of conscription, and in the speculation about possible Government changes. The 1922 Committee, meeting on 20 March with about a hundred Members present, heard Sir Edward Grigg argue the case for compulsory service for one year for youths of nineteen, which on his reckoning would provide an annual intake of about 400,000 men. He considered that unless the Opposition would co-operate, the Conservatives should go to the country on the issue. Mr Leo Amery was among a number of Members supporting compulsory service, but Mr Wise denied that that was the right method. He believed the additional divisions required could be raised within six months under the voluntary system. Sir Henry Page-Croft advocated the compulsory training of all unemployed men. Colonel Heneage claimed that Party divisions on conscription now would give an opportunity to Hitler. Miss Horsbrugh opposed conscription now without an election, and without the widening of the Government. Mr Spens, while in favour of conscription, felt it was necessary to square the Trade Unions first. Another dozen Members joined in an exchange of views, and the *Daily Express* published a colourful report.

At the next meeting of the Committee, on 27 March, Mr Spens raised the question of the 'leaking', and was supported in his complaint by Mr Wise, who referred to other misrepresentations in the press of back-benchers' views, 'all purporting to show unrest among them and a split in the Cabinet'. This led some other Members to raise the suggestion of a 'declaration of secrecy' to be signed by those attending confidential Committee meetings. Sir George Davies recalled similar unhappy occurrences in the past, and Captain Peter Macdonald pointed out that the following night's dinner to the Prime Minister should provide an opportunity to assure him of their confidence. The Chairman, Sir Hugh O'Neill, agreed it was 'a most lamentable state of affairs' but doubted the value of a signed declaration. He thought Members should show their feelings in support of the Prime Minister at the dinner; meanwhile, he would explain to the Chief Whip the inaccuracy of the press reports of last week's meeting.

The dinner, held at the St Stephen's Club on 28 March, and attended by about 170 Members, gave Mr Chamberlain the occasion for an 'emphatic denial that there was any difference of opinion in the Cabinet'.

On 31 March, Mr Chamberlain announced the British guarantee to Poland, and a few weeks later a measure of conscription was carried through Parliament, against the opposition of the Labour and Liberal parties. Meanwhile, Mussolini had invaded Albania; and, before the end of April, Hitler denounced both the Anglo-German Naval Agreement and the German-Polish non-aggression pact. All this was the prelude to the 'Pact of Steel' concluded between Hitler and Mussolini on 22 May, 1939.

At the beginning of May, Mr Frederick Ogilvie, Sir John Reith's successor as Director-General of the BBC, came to the Committee 'and said it was an awkward time to come and address members of the dominant party, because in times of crisis such a party identified itself with the interests of the country which the BBC also tried to serve'.

The BBC regarded it as their duty, when a measure had passed Parliament, to help the Government of the day explain it, and when matters were still controversial to ensure a full discussion. A new step forward had been taken by which, once a month, Parties chose a subject and by whom it should be discussed. He stressed the importance of two other services: (1) to the Empire, on which the BBC were already spending £400,000 a year, and (2) the foreign news service, which now went to eight countries in their own tongue. Those to Germany and Italy were particularly important now. The endeavour was to broadcast truth – no lies, no hatred – and to reflect items which might bring nations together.

This was followed by a reassuring statement, on 8 May, from Admiral of the Fleet, Lord Chatfield, the new Minister of Defence, who thought that 'the organisation of the Committee of Imperial Defence was very efficient' and that 'co-ordination between the three services was real'.

On 12 June, 1939, Dr Burgin, the Minister in charge of the brand new Ministry of Supply, was positively euphoric, declaring that 'the position as regards military requirements was "miles better" than anyone in the room dreamed'.

Curiously, the last two meetings of a session wholly dominated by events in Europe, were devoted to the discussion of developments in Africa and Asia. On 24 July, the Committee listened to the greatest of Colonial Administrators, Lord Hailey, speaking on 'The African Colonies'.

> He disagreed with those who deprecated mining in the Colonies because of its possible adverse effect on the natives, on the grounds that the income from mining provided funds for development in other directions. He thought there should be a Royal Commission to examine the economic resources of the Colonies. On the question of social services, he said that development could not take place without higher grants from Imperial funds. On the political side, he believed that we should consider some extension of local responsibility but not necessarily on the Parliamentary system. On the administrative side, he said that officers were often over-burdened with the detailed work and that it was advisable to create an African subordinate establishment. He considered that officers should not be shifted so often, that amalgamation of areas should be carried through and an African Civil Service set up. He thought it useful to set up an advisory committee of both Houses of Parliament to assist the Colonial Secretary.

On 31 July, 30 members of the 1922 Committee listened to Brigadier-General C. R. Woodroffe's account of his latest visit to China and his journey to Chungking via Indo-China, where he found arms 'pouring in' through Hanoi. He was convinced the Japanese Army was being pinned down, and that if Britain would support Chiang Kai-Shek, with money and aeroplanes, China was bound to win.

On 2 August, Mr Chamberlain moved the formal adjournment of the House until October. But a considerable number of Conservatives, not necessarily committed followers of Churchill or Eden, joined in protesting that there should at least be an assurance that the House would be recalled if any change occurred in the highly volatile situation. When they met again, on 24 August, it was to pass the Emergency Powers Bill, mobilising all reservists and putting the ARP services on the alert. The Nazi-Soviet pact had been signed. On 1 September, Germany invaded Poland. On 3 September, the country and the Committee went to war.

5
The 1922 at War
(1939-45)

THE 1922 COMMITTEE'S FIRST wartime meeting took place on
20 September, 1939, with the Deputy-Chairman, Mr A. A.
Somerville, presiding. He at once announced the resignation of
Sir Hugh O'Neill, who had been appointed an Under-Secretary
of State at the India Office, and of the two Secretaries, Major
Mills and Mr Maurice Petherick, who had gone off to the Army.
It was agreed that the election of a new Chairman should be
taken after the opening of the new Session, and that Mr Emrys
Evans and Mr Hely-Hutchinson should act as Secretaries tem-
porarily. It was also agreed, after two shows of hands, that the
Committee should now meet at 5 p.m. on Wednesdays.

No doubt many of the Members at that first meeting after
war was declared would have liked to come to grips with matters
of high strategy; but after a reference by Major-General Sir
Edward Spears to the danger of the invasion by Germany of
Holland and Belgium and the necessity of calling up more men,
the Committee turned its attention to the comparatively mundane subject of War Risk Insurance on stocks of commodities.
As a result of discussion, Mr Oliver Stanley, who had been
President of the Board of Trade since 1937, attended the next
meeting of the Committee to explain why the Government considered an insurance scheme necessary and why such a scheme
had to be compulsory. He stressed that the real objections to the
scheme nearly all related to the high level of the premium, a level
which his advisers assured him was certainly not too high to
cover the risk involved.

The Committee meeting on 4 October, however, produced a
striking confrontation. Mr Somerville had opened peacefully
enough by asking for the support of the Committee in encourag-

ing work on allotments, when Mr Culverwell, a little-known
Member from Bristol, raised the question of a Secret Session,
saying that he thought the country was drifting to disaster. To
quote from the minutes:

> The Country, in his view, had been stampeded into war by
> the Press, Opposition and Right-Wing Conservatives. Poland
> would never be restored, nor would we break through in
> the West, and the defeat of Germany would mean that
> Europe would become Bolshevik. It was folly to pursue the
> war and we should make peace, recognising Hitler's claim
> to Poland if he offered reasonable terms.

Mr Leo Amery was the first to reply. He supported a Secret
Session, but felt it was most unfortunate that anyone should
hold such views as those Mr Culverwell had expressed: 'The
idea of making peace with Hitler at the present time, after his
victory in Poland, was sheer madness and would have a deplorable effect on the neutrals. The only task before us was the
successful prosecution of the War.' Sir Archibald Southby said
that in his opinion it was wrong to state in advance a refusal to
discuss any peace terms, when these terms had not been
received; but Sir Joseph Lamb, Mr Raikes and Sir John
Wardlaw-Milne were strongly opposed to Mr Culverwell's views,
while Sir Arnold Gridley felt that if they were known in the
Dominions it would create a deplorable effect.

The echoes were still reverberating, however, at the following
week's meeting. Mr Somerville's opening remarks on the necessity for the strictest secrecy, and his reminder of the various
forms enemy propaganda could take, called forth a protest from
Mr Culverwell; but in the general discussion, Mr Amery and
Sir Patrick Hannon raised the banner of free speech in so far
as they wanted the Government ban on public meetings lifted,
and other voices were raised in support of the view that Communist or Fascist propaganda was best countered in the open.
The Committee then turned to a discussion of food rationing.
Members agreed that the first rationing schemes owed too much
to the Civil Service and not enough to practical experience.

A procession of Ministers now came to the Committee to
describe the Government's policy for conducting the war. On
25 October, about two hundred Members attended the Com-

mittee to hear the Foreign Secretary, Lord Halifax. His starting point, naturally enough, was a favourable comparison between the strategical and diplomatic position of Britain at the outbreak of war and what it would have been a year earlier, and he went on to observe that 'probably at any time during the past summer we would have been able to secure an alliance with Russia, if we had been willing to accord her a free hand in the Baltic States'. However, to have done so would have stultified Britain's whole position with regard to aggression, and he considered that, as it was, Germany through her deal with Russia had lost influence politically and strategically in the Balkans and the Ukraine. It might be suggested that logically we should have declared war on Russia; to this he would reply 'first things first'. Our policy must be, if possible, to develop trade with Russia and drive a wedge between her and Germany. Lord Halifax still spoke optimistically about improved relations with Italy, a positive result, he claimed, of Mr Chamberlain's foreign policy. On war aims, he thought it would be a mistake to attempt any detailed definition; peace terms must be governed by what might be possible at the time. With regard to Poland and Czechoslovakia, Britain could only declare she meant to see the wrongs righted, but it was impossible at present to define boundaries. In conclusion, Lord Halifax conceded that real disarmament and a new political and economic world order must be major objectives, but thought it improbable that a large federal organisation of Europe would emerge, though it was possible to hope for a modification of the full application of the principle of national sovereignty.

Lord Halifax was followed at the next meeting by Dr Burgin, the Minister of Supply, whose remarks ranged from the provision of greatcoats to the adequacy of the guns fitted on low-flying aircraft.

A rather brisker approach to the contemporary politico-military scene was provided by Mr Leslie Hore-Belisha, Secretary of State for War, who spoke at the Committee's invitation on 8 November. Again the audience was large, about a hundred and fifty Members, and he opened on a topical note by referring to the peace mediation proposals received that morning from the Queen of the Netherlands and the King of the Belgians. He considered that it was unlikely that neutrals would be willing to provide the sanctions to enforce the terms of any peace. On land it was estimated that the Germans had a superiority in numbers of 3 to 2; but against prepared defensive positions they needed a superiority of 3 to 1 to make a successful attack possible. Mr Hore-Belisha talked of the rapid growth since 1938 in the establishment of the Army's strategic reserves, at home, in the Middle East and in India. Because of the threat of air bombing, the British base was now 50 miles from the front line, on the west coast of France, with GHQ dispersed over a considerable area.

He was followed, on 22 November, by Sir Samuel Hoare, the Chairman of the Home Policy Sub-Committee of the War Cabinet:

He explained that we had made preparations for a hundred per cent air war and that many of the most irksome restrictions arose from this fact. The Government, however, had now been able to relax some of the controls, such as coal rationing, and they were examining the whole problem of lighting regulations. The economic controls were beginning to work much more smoothly, and controls affecting the people's pleasures, such as the restrictions on cinemas and places of entertainment, had been modified.

On 29 November, Mr Anthony Eden, the Dominions Secretary, spoke of the plans for the co-ordination of the Dominions' war effort; he gave a description of the recent visit to France of the Dominions' representatives in London, their reception by M. Daladier, and their tour of the British and French positions.

At the last meeting of the year, the Committee proceeded, as usual, to the election of the Officers and Executive for the new session. There were four nominations for the Chairmanship – Sir Reginald Clarry, Mr W. P. Spens, Sir John Wardlaw-Milne and Sir Joseph Nall.

On the first ballot, Sir Reginald Clarry got closer than ever to the Chairmanship that he had sought for so long. He received 38 votes to the 33 for William Spens. Sir John Wardlaw-Milne, who had played a prominent part in the Indian controversy, and Sir Joseph Nall, a director of a number of transport firms, each received 19 votes. When they both dropped out of the second ballot, Sir Reginald got 60 votes, but William Spens, a short, plump, amiable lawyer with agricultural interests, was elected with 64 votes.

When this domestic business was over, the Committee was addressed by Sir Kingsley Wood, Secretary of State for Air.

As it happened, Sir Kingsley's address was to prove a point of departure from the custom of keeping fairly full records of the weekly meetings. Wartime meetings were often rather rushed affairs and the traditional minutes took some time to read. These were abandoned for the duration of the war. Sir Kingsley mentioned the fact that Germany had refrained from bombing civilians or open towns in France and Britain, and he attributed this not to humanity but to fear of reprisals; he spoke of British superiority in types of planes and personnel, to the growth in numbers of both and the part played by the far-reaching Empire Air Training Scheme.

But when the Committee next met, on 17 January, 1940, the Executive announced that 'in view of the disclosures to the press made following the address by Sir Kingsley Wood, it had been decided that for the period of the war a short summary of proceedings of important meetings of the Committee should be given to the press'. For some time afterwards, the Committee minutes themselves took the form of brief, even tabloid, summaries which might well have been identical with those given to the press. For example, after Mr Churchill's address as First Lord of the Admiralty, on 24 January, the Minute reads:

> The Right Hon. Winston S. Churchill addressed the Committee for over an hour on the Progress and Prospects of the War, from the naval point of view. He illustrated his remarks by diagrams, one showing how the losses at the commencement were mainly due to U-Boats but later to Mines, another showing how at the beginning Great Britain bore the brunt of the losses, but that in the last few weeks an increasing proportion of losses had fallen on neutral shipping.

In the four months that elapsed between Mr Churchill's speech as First Lord and his emergence as Prime Minister, the Committee discussed the serious situation in the building trade; the desirability of reconstituting the War Cabinet, reducing its numbers and freeing its members from departmental duties; the case for appointing a Minister of War Economy; the need for drastic curtailment of imports and problems of foreign exchange; the work of the British Council and of the much-criticised Ministry of Information; and Members also spent considerable time enquiring into the human problems created by the Government's policy towards aliens, and the possible limitation of the Home Secretary's powers in combating subversive activities. The Committee seemed to be adapting itself easily to a wartime routine, but this was soon rudely broken. As the German armed forces over-ran Norway Conservative criticism of the Chamberlain Government mounted. Groups of back-benchers met in committee rooms and clubs to discuss the fate of the administration, but the 1922 Committee was not a forum for these deliberations. Thus on 8 May, the last meeting of the Chamberlain era, a thin audience of 50 listened to the Chancellor of the Exchequer discussing 'the general principles governing the Budget'. On the evening of 8 May the House divided after a two-day debate on the conduct of the war in Norway. Mr Chamberlain's Government had a majority of 81 but 33 members of the 1922 Committee had voted against their colleagues. Those voting with the Opposition included Leo Amery, Robert Boothby, Alfred Duff Cooper and Quintin Hogg, as well as one future prime minister, Harold Macmillan and one future chairman of the 1922 Committee, William Anstruther-Gray. Neville Chamberlain's Government had suffered a mortal blow.

Clearly the creation of a National Coalition Government, under Winston Churchill, marked a turning point for the 1922 Committee. The 1922 Committee had some experience of coalitions after the 1931 General Election, but in those days nine out of every eleven seats on the Government side were held by Conservatives and more than nine-elevenths of the effective power was wielded by Conservative Ministers. In 1940 it was plain that the Socialist ministers in the Coalition Government occupied a number of commanding political heights, while Liberals, and Conservatives of an unorthodox and divisive nature, such as Lord Beaverbrook, had replaced regular Conservatives. There were bound to be suspicions on the part of many members of the 1922 Committee that the new Government was no longer their Government. Nor would it have been surprising if some members of the Committee had misgivings about the future

of their party. After all, the Conservative Party had been divided
by the last wartime coalition and the Liberal Party had been
irreparably broken up by the problems of coalition. It was not
wholly fanciful to believe that the new arrangements could impose
unbearable strains on the Party.

Meanwhile, on a practical, day to day level, there was the
whole problem of creating and maintaining a relationship with
the Labour Party in the House and in the country. An uneasy
party truce had been in existence since September 1939, when
the Chief Whips of the Conservative, Labour and Liberal Parties
had agreed that there should be no contests in Parliamentary by-
elections. It was agreed that the political party which held any
seat that became vacant should be allowed to nominate a new
candidate without opposition; but there had been doubts about
the Labour Party's manoeuvres. Thus, on 15 November, 1939,
Sir Douglas Hacking, the Conservative Party Chairman, had
told the Committee of:

> His anxiety with regard to the position of the Party in
> the constituencies. The Labour Party were doing everything
> in its power to advance its own interests and were using
> the information obtained from Government departments.
> He maintained that we should scrupulously keep the Party
> truce. The Government would, however, be defended and
> the Ministry of Information was supposed to put the case
> for the Government on a broad, national basis. This had not
> been done so far, and the position should be remedied.

But after the formation of Mr Churchill's coalition it seemed
to some Conservative Party members that the Labour Party
was going to get the best of both worlds. On the one hand the
leading Labour Parliamentarians would be Ministers, sharing
in full measure the credit for any success that Mr Churchill's
administration might achieve. On the other hand, Labour Party
members who weren't in the Government still seemed to be
free to carry on the duties of an opposition. This frustration at
seeing the Labour Party gaining at the same time the advantages of both office and opposition led to a degree of pernicketi-
ness on the part of some members of the 1922. There was much
argument about such seemingly trivial points as who should ask
the Leader of the House the question about future business each

week, who should sit on the opposition front bench, and, more importantly, who should have the right to speak immediately before or after Ministers at the opening or closing of a debate.

The full Minutes for the Committee Meeting on 22 May read:

Mr W. Spens in the chair.

Present about 100 members.

> Minutes of the previous Meeting were read and approved.
> Major Sir James Edmondson outlined the business for the week.
> A general discussion took place
> (1) on the allocation among the various Parties of seats on the front Opposition bench,
> (2) on the position in Eire,
> and the Chairman was requested to make representations in the proper quarters as to the views of the Committee.

After the fall of France, there was a natural concentration on home defence and national security. The Committee reverted constantly to such matters as the ventilation of air raid shelters (in the House and outside it), air raid warning systems, discipline in isolated Army posts, civilian morale, the employment of conscientious objectors, and steps to counter harmful propaganda. Among items of business on 31 July occurs the sinister entry: 'Inadequacy of sentences for treason.'

The Ministry of Information was a continuing target of complaint. Like the BBC, it was an irritant to many Committee members though they did not always rationalise their dislike or distrust. Particular resentment was expressed on the subject of meetings arranged in constituencies by the Ministry of Information without the prior knowledge of the sitting Member. But it was not so much the meetings as the Ministry's choice of speakers that offended Tory susceptibilities, and one Minister of Information after another (and the successions were rapid) was at the receiving end of deputations from the Committee.

In August, Mr Spens was requested to convey to Mr Chamberlain a collective expression of the Committee's sympathy in his illness and their hopes for his speedy recovery. His hand-written letter of thanks 'as from No. 11 Downing Street', is pasted in the Minute Book, and was read to the Committee at the next meeting. The Committee had not so far made any formal gesture to Mr Churchill since he became Prime Minister; but in September the Committee spontaneously requested the Chairman to convey to Mr Churchill their 'deep appreciation of the leadership and inspiration which he had given to the country, and especially of the satisfactory arrangements reached with the United States'. The context was the recent agreement for the handing over of 50 elderly American destroyers in return for the lease of air and naval bases to be built on sites in Newfoundland and the Caribbean: an arrangement which proved to be the foundation of the Anglo-American military alliance.

At a later stage, some Members of the Committee lost their enthusiasm for these negotiations. In March 1941, after the terms for the lease of the various base sites had been negotiated with the Americans, Sir Archibald Southby launched a campaign in the Committee to have a debate, in secret session, on the terms. He got some support. Sir Herbert Williams declared that 'there was very grave perturbation in Canada regarding this question'. It was agreed that the Chairman should make strong representations to the Prime Minister through the Chief Whip in favour of such a debate. At that time the Committee was developing a habit of instructing the Chairman to make representations to various Ministers, and this particular mission produced no reaction.

The message of congratulations to Mr Churchill was drawn up at the Committee's first meeting at the new time of 12 noon. On 12 September, the Prime Minister had sent a minute to the Secretary of the War Cabinet, Sir Edward Bridges, referring to the expectation of severe bombing after nightfall. He proposed, *inter alia*: 'to ask Parliament, when it meets at the usual time next Tuesday, to meet in these exceptional circumstances at 11 a.m. and separate at 4 or 5 p.m. This will allow Members to reach their homes, and I hope their shelters, by daylight. We must adapt ourselves to these conditions, which will probably be accentuated.'

These conditions were accentuated. The meeting of the 1922

Committee on 16 October dealt with the rearrangement of future business and sittings of the House, postal delays, priority for MPs on the telephone, use of auxiliary police and troops on the clearing of air-raid debris, and the contribution to be made by mortgage holders towards the premium of air-raid insurance on property. The record concludes: 'It was the sense of the Committee that a debate should be held in secret session on air-raid defence generally, and especially of London.' Churchill, in his memoirs, recalls that the Commons had to be persuaded not to push disregard for their safety too far, but to observe ordinary prudence. 'I convinced them, in Secret Session,' he says, 'of the need to take necessary and well-considered precautions. They agreed that their days and hours of sitting should not be advertised, and to suspend their debates when reports of "Imminent Danger" were made to the Speaker.'* But on 22 October, in another minute to Sir Edward Bridges, Churchill expressed renewed anxiety about alternative accommodation for Parliament:

> The danger to both Houses during their sessions is serious, and it is only a question of time before these buildings and chambers are struck. We must hope they will be struck when not occupied by their Members. The protection provided below the Houses of Parliament is totally inadequate against a direct hit ... I propose to ask for an Adjournment on Thursday next, for a fortnight, by which time it is hoped some plan can be made in London for their meeting.

The first mention of this alternative accommodation, referred to simply as 'The Annexe', occurs in the minutes of the Committee meeting on 11 December. It was there that the election of Officers and Executive was held, bringing Mr Alexander Erskine-Hill into the Chair. Mr Spens had also been nominated, but preferred to withdraw in view of personal difficulty in attending regularly at the mid-day hour which had now been accepted for an indefinite period. There were some members of the Committee who felt that Will Spens was too amiable a man to lead the fight for influence and position which clearly lay

---

* Winston Churchill, *The Second World War*, Vol. II, p. 330 (Cassell & Co. 1949).

before the 1922 Committee. His successor was an equally portly Scottish lawyer, who had been wounded twice while serving in France with the Cameronians in the first World War, and who had a well-developed taste for political combat on and off the main stage. Neither of the Secretaries who had acted *pro tem* wished to carry on, and these posts were filled by Mr John Crowder and Mr Allan Chapman. The latter suggested that a woman should be co-opted onto the Executive, and Lady Davidson, the wife of Sir John Davidson who had been Chairman of the Party in the 1922 Committee's early days, agreed to serve. But a proposal by Sir Reginald Clarry (who with Sir Annesley Somerville remained Vice-Chairman) that the Chairman should retire every year and not be eligible for re-election for twelve months, proved too revolutionary and was withdrawn – and with it went Sir Reginald's last chance of becoming Chairman himself.

The Committee's last business in 1940 was to recommend 'that the Prime Minister be approached with a view to his attending a luncheon in the New Year, and that the Ministry of Food be consulted regarding the menu'.

Meanwhile, Mr Churchill gave the Committee something unpleasant to chew upon at the end of 1940. The new Chairman, Mr Erskine-Hill, reported to a meeting of the Executive that the Chief Whip had informed him that the Prime Minister contemplated asking Cabinet Ministers not to address Party Committees such as the 1922 Committee. The record merely states that 'strong opposition to this suggestion was expressed by all the Members present', and goes on to record the decision to invite Lord Beaverbrook, a member of the War Cabinet, and Minister of Aircraft Production, to address the Committee at an early date.

This particular issue coincided with a change of Chief Whips, and provided a difficult debut for the new Chief Whip, James Stuart. Over the nine years that Captain David Margesson had been Chief Whip, Conservative back-benchers had grown accustomed to his firm ways. *The Times* had described him as follows: 'Lean, dark, elegant and strikingly handsome, David Margesson was a man of forceful personality and he was often spoken of as having been the most powerful Chief Whip since the Master

of Elibank in the Liberal Government of 1906. He was dicta-
torial, even ruthless, in his methods ... in the military tradition
that had moulded him he was a rigid disciplinarian.'

David Margesson had been adjutant of the 11th Hussars and
had won a Military Cross in the first World War. James Stuart
continued this military tradition. He had won an MC on the
Somme, and had become adjutant of the Second Battalion of the
Royal Scots at the age of 19.

In December 1938, James Stuart had had a sharp clash with
Winston Churchill over the Perthshire by-election. The Duchess
of Atholl had resigned her seat after a disagreement with the
Government, and her local Conservative Association, over foreign
policy. She fought the by-election as an Independent against an
official Conservative candidate, and Winston Churchill had sent
her a telegram of support.

The Duchess lost by 1,313 votes, but the Churchill telegram
angered the local Conservatives. James Stuart's rebuke was not
well received.

Just two years later James Stuart became Winston Churchill's
Chief Whip in a dual capacity. He was not only Chief Whip of
the Conservative Party, he was also Chief Whip of a National
Government containing Labour Ministers. The two roles might
well clash as the instruction about Cabinet Ministers appearing
at the 1922 Committee suggested.

When he had become Chief Whip, James Stuart was asked
whether he intended to continue the firm Margesson tradition,
and he had replied that he did not intend to try and out-Herod
Herod. On the question of Cabinet appearances, James Stuart
met the Committee more than half-way. Mr Erskine-Hill was
able to tell the Executive, immediately after the Christmas recess,
that he had seen the Chief Whip and it had been agreed 'that
the present procedure of Ministers being asked to address the
Committee should continue, but that an "all party" meeting
should be held occasionally'. The Chairman and one of the joint
Secretaries were deputed to make the necessary arrangements
and were authorised to meet the representatives of other parties
as required.

This episode seems to have been kept within the circle of
the Executive, as no reference to it is recorded in the minutes
of the main committee. It could be interpreted as showing how

far the preoccupations of war had removed the consideration of
party politics from Churchill's mind and how determined he was
that his national leadership should not be impeded by party
obstacles such as the possible implication of Conservative privilege. It also reveals the awareness of the Committee's elected
leaders that they had the power to contest Prime Ministerial
decisions – provided there was the will. Had the Executive failed
the Committee could have taken an important step backwards
in influence. As it was, Cabinet Ministers in great variety continued to address the Committee, the first in 1941 being Lord
Beaverbrook, who assured Members in the course of his speech
that 'perfect harmony existed between his colleagues and himself'.
The Committee could also take satisfaction from the fact that
the new Chief Whip, Mr Stuart, at his meeting with the Committee on 29 January, went out of his way to emphasise continuity with his predecessors in expressing his wish to co-operate
in every possible way, a wish the Committee reciprocated.

Nevertheless, it was not always easy to be content with the
meagre diet which was all that the wartime rationing of politics
allowed back-benchers – at any rate, the Tory majority. The
fare was sufficient to sustain life, but it was often unappetising,
and the hunger for something more satisfactory could not always
be contained. Irritation over such relatively mundane matters as
Local Authority Grants for shelters, the difficulty of obtaining
information from the Regional Commissioners, arguments over
the rates of pay for fire-watchers, all owed something to the
increasing spread of Government bureaucracy and the corresponding decrease in the individual MPs status and authority,
even in his own constituency. Conservatives were particularly
irked by the feeling that Central Office propaganda appeared to
lie fallow, while speakers of left-wing sympathies proliferated on
the platforms provided by the Ministry of Information and the
BBC. That was the view of many critics in the 1922 Committee
in the spring of 1941. No doubt it played a part in the decision
reached after Sir Douglas Hacking, the Party Chairman, had
come to the Committee in March, to appoint a liaison committee
of members of the 1922 to work in close touch with Conservative Central Office. Its members were: Mr Erskine-Hill, Sir
George Davies, Mr Oliver Simmonds, Mr John Crowder, and
later Colonel Evans, Sir Derrick Gunston and Mr Kenneth

Pickthorn. Nor was the Minister of Information let off lightly at the meeting he addressed a few weeks later. Questions put to Mr Duff Cooper, the current holder of that well-nigh impossible post (he had been preceded by Lord Macmillan and Sir Sir John Reith, and was shortly to be succeeded by Mr Brendan Bracken) ranged from censorship and home security, to the staffing of regional Information Offices and the direction of foreign broadcasts.

An occasional fanfare was needed, and this was supplied on 26 March, when Mr Churchill was the guest of the Committee at a luncheon at the Savoy. More than 150 Members were present (the charge 10s a head, exclusive of wines) and Mr Erskine-Hill presided. *The Times'* parliamentary correspondent reported:

> The Prime Minister was given a great reception. When he said, in the course of his speech, 'we shall let no Party surpass us in the great sacrifices we make', his audience showed that they fully shared his sentiment.
>
> In proposing Mr Churchill's health, the Chairman said, amid cheers: 'The Prime Minister has ridden the ill-winds of circumstance and has snatched the beginning of victory from seeming defeat ...'

From late April to late June 1941, the Committee was again transacting its business in the 'Annexe', a reflection of the series of very heavy raids on London, including the heavy damage suffered by the House of Commons on 10 May, but a change of location did not change the Committee's temper. Thus, on 28 May, 1941, the Minutes record:

> *Mr Pickthorn* suggested that some machinery should be set up for reporting on Bills, Regulations and Draft Orders before they were brought before the House. Several members supported this suggestion and it was decided that the Chief Whip should approach the Chairman of the Party with a view to obtaining assistance from the Central Office.
>
> It was also agreed that the Liaison Committee should also ask Sir Douglas Hacking to meet them to discuss the matter.

It was proposed that *Mr Pickthorn* should join the Committee. This was agreed to.

Major Lloyd referred to the maladministration of the Ministry of Labour with special reference to the increasing lack of discipline amongst the dockers of Clydeside.

Members were asked to send any information in their possession to Major Lloyd.

Sir Percy Hurd raised the question of the 'snooping' activities of the Ministry of Information.

Professor Savory referred to the refusal of the Government to impose conscription on Northern Ireland.

Sir James Edmondson was asked to report to the Chief Whip.

Sir George Davies suggested that the British Israel World Federation Movement should be carefully watched, as he thought it was spreading a certain amount of dissatisfaction in many people's minds regarding the prosecution of the War.

Mr Strauss asked Members to support him in resisting an attempt by the Ministry of Aircraft Production to disfigure a certain part of the country by erecting permanent buildings for employees as part of a housing scheme. He pointed out that this was being done in spite of an assurance in writing given by the Parliamentary Secretary.

It was agreed that a deputation should see Sir John Anderson after the recess on the general question of the machinery in Government departments which made it possible for such things to happen.

Throughout the spring and early summer of 1941, there came constant complaints about low productivity and indiscipline among organised labour, and on 2 July, 1941, Mr Ernest Bevin, Minister of Labour, became the first Socialist Cabinet Minister to address the full Committee.

The circumstances of Mr Ernest Bevin's visit were, on the face of it, not very favourable. He and his Ministry had been under criticism for some time both in the Committee and on the floor of the House, and resentment was especially aroused by a speech of Mr Bevin's at Birmingham in April, in which he was felt to have made a personal attack on three local Conservative Members. The matter was raised in the Committee and, as a result, the Chairman was requested to see the Prime Minister so as to make Members' views known. In June, particular complaints were made in the Committee of failure to deal with indiscipline in the docks, and of a lag in industrial output generally. It was said that boys of 14 were being paid £5 a week for work on aerodromes. The Essential Works order also came under attack for diminishing the employers' powers of dismissal. Again, it was proposed to send a deputation to the Prime Minister; but, after further discussion, it was decided that Mr Bevin should first be invited to address the Committee. About a hundred and twenty Members attended to hear him, on 2 July; but Mr Bevin preferred to leave most of the talking to his audience, and after a short statement in explanation of the Essential Works Order, he asked for questions. These came thick and fast. The following are taken from the Minutes:

> Sir John Mellor on absenteeism in aircraft factories; Wing-Commander James on high wages paid to labour employed on aerodrome construction; Mr Radford on piece-work rates which he understood enabled semi-skilled men to earn more than the highly-skilled; Major Lloyd on alleged indiscipline on Clydeside; Mr Summers on dilution; Colonel Evans on woman-power and the competition with the Services in recruitment; Mr Levy on low production in the building and mining industries; Mr Nunn on the need to prevent contractors 'holding men not fully employed'; and Sir Frederick Sykes on welfare and canteen work among miners.

After the Minister had left, 'the Chairman asked if Members still wished to send a deputation to the Prime Minister. After some discussion, it was decided to postpone the matter for the time being.' And there it rested.

After the comparative success of Ernest Bevin's visit, an invitation was quickly extended to the leader of the Labour Party, Clement Attlee. As Lord Privy Seal and acting Leader of the House of Commons, Mr Attlee's subject, on 16 July, was the general working of the War Cabinet, stressing in particular that points raised there were not discussed on party lines, but always in the general interest of the community. He also pointed out that there would be great problems to face after the war, and that party differences 'must not be allowed to interfere with post-war reconstruction'. This counsel of perfection was not challenged on the spot, but as time passed, there was a strong feeling in the Committee that the protagonists of 'creeping Socialism' were exploiting the wartime party truce which Conservatives, however reluctantly, continued to observe in the country at large.

The jaundiced eyes of certain Committee Members continued to keep the personnel of the Government under critical review. Thus, on 23 July, 1941, it is recorded that:

> *Mr Orr-Ewing* raised the question of the new Government appointments, especially as regards Mr Duff Cooper, Mr Thurtle and Mr Sandys. He viewed the last appointment with some dissatisfaction.
>
> *Mrs Tate* thought that the appointment of Mr Thurtle would have a serious effect on the country as he was a professing Atheist.
>
> *Mr Nunn* thought the appointment of Mr Duff Cooper was a dangerous one.

In the latter half of the year, the Committee was concerned in two more substantial controversies. These were the TUC request to amend the Trade Disputes Act of 1927, and allegations of defects in the design of the Churchill tank.

The Trade Disputes Act and the memory of the fate of Macquisten's Bill had become part of the folk-lore of the 1922 Committee. The proposal to amend it provoked an immediate closing of the ranks. The matter came up at a meeting on 10 September, 1941, when Mr Erskine-Hill revealed a proposal whereby the Executive Committee of the National Union was to appoint seven Conservatives to meet an equal number of TUC representatives, to hear details of their request to amend the Act. Arising from this, he recalled that at a meeting some months earlier with Sir John Anderson, the Lord President of the Council, he had been told that any proposal to amend the Act would be reported to the 1922 Committee. It had been, but in a roundabout way, and Members did not like it. While some conceded that the TUC could not be refused the opportunity to put forward their case, other members thought that the Committee should let it be known 'they would not tolerate' any amendment. Eventually, it was agreed that the Whip attending the Committee should inform his chief of the Committee's views as follows:

1. That they trusted the Executive of the Party would instruct its seven nominees that they should hear the views of the TUC representatives, ask any questions to elucidate those views and should then report back; and that they should not be given any authority to negotiate or reach any agreement.
2. That the 1922 Committee would not be bound in any way by anything done without its express authorisation.

The sensitivity of the Committee on this subject was again apparent at the meeting on 1 October, when Colonel Gretton read a paragraph from a recent issue of *The Times*, which was felt to give the impression that the leaders of the Liberal Party were to be kept informed of progress in the discussions between Tories and TUC regarding the proposal to amend the Act. The Deputy Chief Whip, Major Dugdale, who was attending the Committee, explained that the Prime Minister had only agreed that a report of the *result* of the discussions would be given to Sir Archibald Sinclair.

The sequel to the episode was furnished, so far as the TUC was concerned, by Sir Walter Citrine, in a report to the Trade Union Congress nearly a year later. He said that at the suggestion of the Government, the General Council had had a meeting with representatives of the Conservative Party, but had found them 'entirely unresponsive'. Since then he had received a letter from the Prime Minister, asking him strongly, in the national interest, to refrain from pressing the matter at the present critical time.

In November, Mr Erskine-Hill was re-elected Chairman of the Committee, unopposed; Sir Reginald Clarry and Sir Annesley Somerville continued their run as Vice-Chairmen; and Colonel Gretton became Treasurer. At this meeting, Mr Erskine-Hill reported that the Deputy Leader of the Labour Party had given him leave to say that the Labour Party was willing to co-operate with the Conservatives in setting up a committee, to arrange meetings in the country under the auspices of the

Ministry of Information with the object of promoting enthusiasm for further aid to Russia. This was a gesture impossible to imagine a few months back, and one which, in the present context, it was impossible to ignore. Moreover, it opened up the prospect of exerting some Tory influence on the selection of speakers which many Members of the 1922 had long felt to be far too partial towards the Left. At any rate, the co-operation went forward and early in the New Year – the year of agitation for a Second Front – an all-party committee was duly formed charged, among other tasks, with choosing speakers for all 'Aid for Russia' meetings held under Ministry auspices.

The suggestion of dissatisfaction with the performance of the Churchill tank first came up in the Committee on 10 December, 1941. Mr Hammersley asked whether an early debate in secret might be arranged in order to discuss tank production generally, and the Churchill tank in particular. He followed this up with an account of defects in the tank which caused considerable alarm. That there was genuine unease is clear from the Chairman's suggestion that as a first step, a deputation should be appointed to see Lord Beaverbrook, now Minister of Supply, and Captain Margesson, the Secretary of State for War, immediately. It was agreed that it should be left to the deputation to decide, after the interview with the Ministers, whether to demand a Secret Session. A week later, the Committee heard that the deputation had seen Lord Beaverbrook, Captain Margesson, and Mr Lucas, a technical expert. Lord Beaverbrook had said steps were already being taken in the matter and the Committee would be kept in touch with progress in remedying the defects.

Clearly, the 1922 Committee was not competent to pass any sort of technical judgement on the Churchill tank or any other major item of equipment, but Members did have widespread contacts. Mr Hammersley, for example, had served with the Tank Corps in the First World War, and had maintained close links with his old comrades. Every Member had relatives or close friends serving in the armed forces, and by the end of 1941, almost a hundred Members of Parliament, ranging in rank from Admiral-of-the-Fleet Sir Roger Keyes to Private Sir Richard Acland, combined military service with intermittent attendance at Parliament.

Not every Member was competent to talk about tanks, but

few could resist the temptation to discuss the wider strategic
direction of the war. There were plenty of Members ready to
give their advice when the military situation deteriorated shortly
after Japan entered the war on 7 December, 1941.

At a meeting on 18 February, 1942, Mr Culverwell (who had
taken so jaundiced a view of the decision to declare war in 1939)
got considerable support when he spoke of dissatisfaction with
the present position, and suggested there was need for drastic
changes in the Government. Flight-Lieutenant Raikes thought
it a mistake for the Prime Minister also to hold the Defence
Portfolio, but Mr Strauss doubted whether the remedy was a
divorce of the two offices. He advocated a War Cabinet of men
'of at least average ability' to criticise war plans and advise
generally; he would like all the present Ministers to place their
resignations in the hands of the Prime Minister, leaving him a
free hand in selecting men of the highest calibre, irrespective of
Party. Sir Cuthbert Headlam felt the three Service Ministers
should be in the War Cabinet. Sir Arnold Gridley disagreed.
He thought it a waste of time to argue whether the Prime Minister
should keep the Defence Ministry, since any Prime Minister
must always carry responsibility for defence measures; rather,
the Committee should concentrate on trying to persuade Mr
Churchill to appoint another Deputy Leader of the House. He
also pointed out there was widespread feeling that the Board of
Admiralty should be strengthened by the inclusion of younger
men.

One did not have to be a potential member of the War Cabinet
to see that the advance of the Japanese added a threat of physical
invasion to the continuing undercurrent of political unrest in
India. The question of a political initiative there was raised in
the Committee on 4 March by Sir Stanley Reed, who had a
long association with Indian affairs. His suggestion that interested
Members should discuss the situation in anticipation of a
Government statement led to the calling of a special meeting on
the following day. The Secretary of State for India, Mr L. S.
Amery, was present.

Mr Amery did not, of course, disclose the content of the
proposals about to be made to the Indian leaders; but the
Committee's special meeting provided a means of sounding-out
back-bench opinion in view of the 1940 pledge to India of full

Dominion status after the war. Among those who spoke in the Committee, Sir George Jefferies hoped the Government's proposals would not be interpreted as appeasement of Congress, which he considered to be as much anti-British as anti-Muslim; he was doubtful whether there should be any drastic alteration in the existing administration of India in the middle of the war. Lord Winterton felt armed revolt was possible if the attempt was made to put Muslims under Hindu rule. Most of the subsequent speakers, including Will Spens who was soon to go to India as Chief Justice, were apprehensive of a 'deal' with the Congress Party, and some expressed anxiety as to Indian willingness to fight unless more was done to encourage the pro-British elements, whether Hindu or Muslim. It was evident, however, that while the future of India was still an emotional issue, the outlook of many Members was now more tolerant of change than in the heated debate within the party of the thirties.

Soon after the discussion on India, the Committee mourned the death of its senior Vice-Chairman, Sir Annesley Somerville, who had been born during the Indian Mutiny. For about forty years before his first election to Parliament, he had been a schoolmaster of rare distinction and for almost twenty years within the Committee and the Executive he had contributed a magisterial note to the discussion.

Sir Annesley Somerville's successor as Vice-Chairman of the 1922 Committee was Sir Arnold Gridley, and there can be no doubt that the great fuel debate of 1942 led to Sir Arnold's elevation.

The coal problem had been worrying the Government for some years. When war was declared in September 1939, a Fuel and Lighting Order had been issued, which required domestic and small industrial consumers to restrict their consumption of coal, gas and electricity to 75% of the amounts consumed or acquired in the corresponding quarter of the year which ended in June 1939. In fact, fuel consumption was not as heavy as had been expected and the restrictions were relaxed in November 1939.

The possibility of rationing the domestic consumer was not raised again until the summer of 1941, when the authorities began to feel some concern about the fuel stocking position for the winter of 1941-2. A fuel-saving publicity campaign was launched and the civil service began to give some thought to the preparation of a general ration scheme. It had been estimated that the consumption and production of coal would remain in rough balance up until the summer of 1942, at an annual rate of 207 million tons a year. But consumption of gas and electricity was increasing rapidly, and the planners estimated that demand for 1942-3 would reach 215 million tons without any substantial increase in production. The original rationing plans envisaged a saving of about six million tons of coal a year on the domestic side.

On 17 March, 1942, the recently-appointed President of the Board of Trade, Mr Hugh Dalton, told the House of Commons that the production of coal was insufficient and consumption excessive. It was imperative to build up stocks as from the autumn, and it was therefore proposed to introduce a 'comprehensive scheme of fuel rationing' as soon as possible. There was as yet no particular alarm or despondency; but on 21 April, 1942, Mr Dalton revealed that the scheme, applying to coal, gas and electricity, would operate on a points system with interchangeable coupons. It would be complex and expensive and an extra 15,000 temporary clerks would be required. Nevertheless, the Government was satisfied that the scheme, based on a report specially prepared by Sir William Beveridge, should go ahead.

The problem was not a simple one. By 1942, the systems of rationing for food and clothing were well established, but as the official historian of the coal industry at war, Professor W. H. B. Court, has pointed out: 'the equitable distribution of fuel is by the nature of the case a more difficult matter than the fair sharing of food or even of clothing ... Stomachs are so much more alike than buildings ... the rationing of fuel ... would certainly have been the most difficult of all the rationing plans to administer.'[*]

Sir Arnold Gridley took the lead when the matter was discussed at a committee meeting on 22 April. The main objection from the first was the vast organisation required to administer the points and coupons system. He pointed out that there would have to be something like 12 million assessments, entailing a huge staff and the issue of millions of coupon books. The

---

[*] W. H. B. Court, *Official History of the Second World War* (vol. on Coal), p. 161 (HM Stationery Office and Longmans).

rationing of gas and electricity he regarded as impracticable, but in the case of coal he was certain the way to tackle the problem was more production. If production could be increased by 5% all would be well, and he blamed the Government for not bringing more men back to the mines or not dealing more effectively with absenteeism. Mr Dalton, in fact, had already had a rough ride in the House, not so much on the necessity of rationing – though that was disputed – as on the method proposed. Criticism was enhanced by the publication of Sir William Beveridge's report on 28 April, so that when Mr Dalton came to the Committee on the 30th, the full plan was open to attack.

Mr Dalton did not present a wholly inflexible attitude. He stressed the increasing demands of the war effort and industry, the effect on morale in poor homes if a means of equitable distribution of fuel were not found, and the possibility of having to send coal to the Middle East, Northern Russia, Canada and even to South Africa. But he said, too, that the Government did not accept all the details of the Beveridge scheme, and that it would welcome concrete suggestions. The matter could not be delayed, and he reminded the Committee that many Utility Companies had been left with only two weeks' supply early in 1942. On manpower, he said the Government still held that no miners could be released from combat units, but some might be taken from supply formations: a total of 11,000 miners had been released from the Services and essential industry.

After the Minister had left, a general discussion took place. Conflicting views emerged as to the practicability of releasing more miners from the forces, but the Committee was firmly agreed that drastic steps to increase coal production must go hand in hand with equitable distribution. Arnold Gridley was again the chief protagonist of an alternative scheme, and the Committee issued the following statement to the press:

The President of the Board of Trade addressed the 1922 Committee today, at a special meeting at which over 120 Members were present, when he fully explained the need for a fuel rationing scheme, both in the interests of economy and of equitable distribution, and invited any constructive suggestions.

After answering a considerable number of questions, Mr

Dalton left the meeting, which proceeded to discuss his statement.

The Committee were unanimous as to the urgent need both for economy in consumption and for measures of ensuring an equitable distribution of coal, gas and electricity; and also as to the drastic need to increase coal production.

They, however, felt that a simpler scheme could be worked out with the assistance of the industries concerned which would avoid coupons and all the costly administrative staff envisaged by the Beveridge proposals.

Such a scheme would take some days to formulate, and the Committee felt it would be preferable that no debate on the scheme as at present outlined should take place until time had been given for the formation of an alternative.

The Committee next met on 6 May, the eve of the Commons debate on the Government's proposals. Meanwhile, Sir Arnold Gridley had seen Mr Dalton, and had also been in touch with the coal owners, with some of the distributors and with the heads of the Gas and Electricity undertakings. He reported that everyone he had spoken to was 'very much against' any scheme involving coupons. He suggested that Members should make clear that they would not support any 'coupon scheme'. This received the Committee's overwhelming support, and the Executive then approved a further press notice:

Another largely attended meeting of the 1922 Committee was held today. Members discussed in some detail alternatives to the Beveridge scheme for the reduction of domestic consumption of fuel. It was the overwhelming opinion of those present that the production of coal could and should be increased immediately.

Members were emphatic in their objection to any scheme of rationing involving the use of coupons on a points system or otherwise, but agreed that consumption must be reduced.

After the debate on 7 May, the storm broke. This was brought about, in part, by the impression – despite Mr Dalton's fair words – that the Government intended to hurry on with the essence of the Beveridge scheme, and also by the cold reception given by Sir Stafford Cripps, who wound up the debate, to Sir Arnold Gridley's alternative. This had envisaged coal, coke and paraffin rationing by distributors, with the consumption of gas and electricity cut down by means of penal charges on any excess over a given quantity. Sir Stafford dismissed this as providing golden opportunities for a 'black market' in coal and coke. He concluded by saying that a White Paper containing the Government's definitive plans would be published in a few days.

This did not happen, and some of the reasons why are to be found in the records of the Committee's meeting on 13 May. At this meeting the Chairman, Mr Erskine-Hill, informed the Committee that he had seen the Lord Privy Seal and the President of the Board of Trade on 8 May, and had told them that Sir Stafford Cripps' speech on the previous day had misrepresented Members' views. As the misrepresentation continued, he had written a letter to the *Sunday Times*, 'although as a general rule he thought it inadvisable for the Chairman of the 1922 Committee to rush into print'. His action had been unanimously endorsed by the Executive Committee. It met some criticism, however, in the main Committee from Sir Derrick Gunston, who thought it was creating a dangerous precedent for the Committee to give the impression that they were bringing pressure to bear on the Government, while Lord Winterton also had some reservations. A vote of confidence in Mr Erskine-Hill was then carried unanimously.

The letter in the *Sunday Times* of 10 May declared:

Sir,

The Leader of the House of Commons, Sir Stafford Cripps, in winding up the debate on fuel rationing, may unintentionally have created a wrong impression to the House of Commons and to the country as to the attitude of the Conservative Members on this very vexed question.

Your readers will recall that the 1922 Committee, of which I have the honour to be Chairman, issued a strong statement to the press last Wednesday affirming their emphatic objections to any scheme which involves coupons and points rationing. I fully believe that this attitude is one which the householders of this country would wish their representatives to take.

Fuel must be conserved in the national interest, but the nation neither needs nor desires a points rationing scheme, nor the imposition upon the taxpayer of new hordes of officials. A personal appeal from the Prime Minister would go very far to secure the results required, and an alternative scheme, such as the one recommended to the House by Sir Arnold Gridley, would further strengthen the position and ensure that the wrongdoers would be penalised.

The Mines Department must have appreciated the position for some months, and cannot use its own delays as an excuse for stampeding the country into a complicated scheme which would materially add to the ranks of the bureaucrats.

Mr Erskine-Hill's letter provoked, among other comment, an acid editorial in the *Daily Herald* interpreting the Committee's stand against fuel rationing as an attempt to 'intimidate' the Government. This in turn gave rise to an astringent analysis in the *Daily Telegraph* of Labour's own assertion of the right to oppose while not hesitating to use 'intimidation' tactics against their own non-conforming Members. The *Herald* also issued a challenge, suggesting that Tory MPs should go down a coal mine during the recess. On a show of hands in Committee, it was revealed that 84% of the Members present (100) had already been down a mine.

The campaign was not closed, as the continuing discussion in the Committee showed. Sir Arnold Gridley asked whether the Committee was prepared to oppose rationing if the Government introduced a scheme such as Beveridge proposed? He said that Ministers and the coal trade were agreed that restriction was necessary. He had met Sir Stafford Cripps, Mr Dalton, Sir William Beveridge and their advisers on 9 May, and they had met representatives of the coal trade a day or so later. These representatives had asserted that the Beveridge scheme was unworkable, and had handed in an alternative, based on the same principles as his own, even the Co-operative Society agreed with him. Sir Arnold had informed Sir Stafford Cripps and Mr Dalton that if they persisted in ignoring the advice which had been proffered them, he and those who agreed with him would vote against the Government. He welcomed the Chairman's letter to the *Sunday Times* as Mr Dalton was under the impression that the Party was divided on this question. The Government should know where the Committee stood. As Professor Court has noted:

It was publicly known that coal supplies were such that production could hardly be left to be carried on as it was; some sort of Government control was presumably in the offing. The question became mixed up with feeling against the Government control of industry, which was beginning to make itself keenly felt. The rationing plan became a sort of unacknowledged test of the relative strength of parties and interests within the Coalition Government and in Parliament, behind a barrage of arguments about its administrative virtues and defects.*

The Chairman undertook to call a special meeting of the Committee as soon as the Government scheme was made known. Meanwhile, he himself had another interview with Sir Stafford Cripps, and the Government decided to give itself more time before issuing the White Paper originally expected before Whitsun. This was published on 3 June, and showed that much reliance was to be placed on voluntary restriction by consumers. The Committee held its special meeting next day, but Sir Arnold and others were still suspicious that though rationing was held in abeyance, it might be brought in in unforeseen circumstances without the Commons' prior approval. This point was met in the debate on 10 June, during the second reading of the Bill embodying the Government's modified proposals. The piloting of the Bill was entrusted to Sir John Anderson, the Lord President, who undertook that the Government would not introduce rationing without giving the House the opportunity of further debate if desired. It had been a notable engagement, in which the Committee achieved its major objective – no coupons, and no points system. The statistical record would seem to justify the Committee's campaign. The proposed rationing scheme was scrapped and the threatened coal crisis did not materialise.

* Court, *op. cit.*, pp. 160-1.

Although there had been Conservative members of the Cabinet Committee dealing with the rationing issue, the main burden of the debate had been borne by the two Socialist Ministers least popular with the Committee as a whole. In particular, Sir Stafford Cripps was regarded with suspicion. Curiously, Sir Stafford's Parliamentary Private Secretary was a Conservative, Mr G. E. Palmer, a member of the biscuit-making family, who, according to his biographical notes, had 'set himself to learn the practice and principles of politics'. The controversy had been highly educational. On 10 June, Palmer reported to the Committee that:

A few Members had raised with him the question as to the nature of the Reports which he gave to his Minister in the Committee regarding the proceedings of the Committee.

He said that he only conveyed the general view of the Party to the Lord Privy Seal, and did not give details of who spoke or what was actually said. He hoped the Committee would have confidence in his judgement as to what he reported to his Minister.

On 8 July, 'The Chairman announced that it had been agreed that Mr Palmer should continue to act as Sir Stafford Cripps' PPS; that he should use his own discretion in reporting to him, but that no names of Members should be mentioned or reference made to purely Party matters.'

There was a less amicable outcome to the meeting on 30 June, 1942. Sir John Wardlaw-Milne, a Committee stalwart for many years, was due to open a vote of censure on the Government in the House, on the motion 'That this House, while paying tribute to the heroism and endurance of the Armed Forces of the Crown, in circumstances of exceptional difficulty, has no confidence in the central direction of the War'. The Minutes record that:

A discussion took place on the debate of Sir John Wardlaw-Milne's Motion, in which about 30 Members took part. It was agreed that the press should be informed that the discussion had taken place and that the overwhelming majority were agreed that the Motion was ill-advised and should not be supported.

In the event, after a debate in which Sir John had called
for the appointment of the Duke of Gloucester as Commander-
in-Chief of the British Army, the censure motion was defeated
by 476 to 25. Among those voting against the Government were
Aneurin Bevan, Sir Herbert Williams, Sidney Silverman, and
Admiral-of-the-Fleet Sir Roger Keyes.

Sir John Wardlaw-Milne would certainly have attracted more
votes if he had moved a vote of censure criticising the Prime
Minister's handling of Parliament or of the Government's
relations with Conservative back-benchers.

Public opinion testing was still in its infancy, but there were
ominous signs that support for the Conservative Party was
declining in the country. In March 1942, an Independent candidate running with some unofficial support from the local Labour
Party won a by-election in the supposedly safe Conservative
seat at Grantham.

At the time of the Grantham reversal, the war seemed to be
going badly on many fronts, but even the steady improvement
in the military situation which followed the harnessing and
growth of the vast American war machine did nothing to ease
tensions in Parliament. In 1940, when the German threat was
close and fierce, it was understandable that back-benchers should
acquiesce readily in the passage of emergency legislation which
increased enormously the power of the Executive. But when it
seemed that the German threat had been checked, it was understandable that there should be a growing feeling that the powers
of the Executive should be scrutinised more closely. It was
equally natural that the Executive should not welcome this
development.

Meanwhile, all the old feelings that the Labour Party was
getting an unfair advantage in many small but important matters
of privilege and procedure continued to rankle. An exchange
of letters between the Chairman of the 1922 Committee and
the Chief Whip, in May 1942, has been preserved:

27 May 1942

Dear James,

I have had a large number of complaints regarding the
Chair's calling of Labour Members in preference to our
own people in the last two days' debate. I have no doubt

you will have had some representations to this effect. Apart from the Government speakers, Labour or Liberal speakers both opened and closed the debate on both days. The effect of the opening and closing speeches together with the speeches of those whom the Speaker called was that an entirely false impression of the feeling of the House was created. A great many speakers, including Willink and Pickthorn were extremely anxious to support the Prime Minister and attack the line taken by Clem Davies, Wardlaw-Milne and Belisha.

There is a growing feeling of resentment in the Party that Greenwood should present to the Speaker a list of people who are called as a matter of course, whereas our people just have to take their chance, and that in spite of what we all recognise you do to get our fellows in.

I am informed the matter is going to be raised at the 22 Committee at our first meeting. It might be advisable for us to have a talk before this.

Yours,
A. G. ERSKINE-HILL

James Stuart replied quickly:

I have received your letter of 27 May, and I am aware of the feeling aroused as a result of the order in which speakers were called and of the number of speakers from the respective parties during the last debate on the Conduct of the War.

I have taken the matter up once again with the Labour Party in order that Conservative feeling on the subject may be realised in that quarter, and I am assured by Whiteley that – with the exception of their official opening and closing speakers – no list is given to the Chair and that other speakers have to take their chance in the ordinary way.

I am most anxious to avoid the impression being created that Labour has a right to open or close a particular debate, and in this instance I did urge that Ned Grigg, who, as you know, was a prime mover in the demand for a discussion on Joint Planning, should open. He, however, was anxious to avoid speaking during the luncheon hour and eventually seemed to prefer getting in a little later, as he did. Part of the unfortunate impression was, of course, caused by a fact that neither of the Government speakers was a Conservative.

While I know you have not suggested that I should present a list of speakers from our side to the Chair, I do hope that Members will not suggest that I should be pressed to interfere with the Chair in this matter. Apart from the fact that it is the responsibility of the Chair to see that a debate is properly conducted and well balanced, it would obviously place me in a hopeless position if everyone who wished to speak came to the Whips' Office and left it to us to hand a list to the Speaker. The displeasure of anyone who was not called would naturally be vented upon me in every case, and I think that my position would become untenable.

I shall be glad to see you on the subject and I hope that you will give me a ring on Monday some time.

The issue remained alive during the summer and autumn, with continued minor complaints recorded in the minutes. Beverley Baxter spoke for many Members when he declared that in his opinion 'the Labour Party had agreed to co-operate in the war at the price of the abdication of the Conservative Party'.

On 8 September, 1942, Mr Churchill opened a debate on the military situation. There was some confusion about the whipping and by the time that Mr Arthur Greenwood, the Labour Party spokesman, was near the end of his speech from the front bench there were barely twenty Members left in the Chamber. The day's debate died through lack of speakers, and in reply to a question, Sir Stafford Cripps, the Leader of the House, passed this sharp comment: 'I do not think that we can conduct our proceedings here with the dignity and the weight with which we should conduct them unless Members are prepared to pay greater attention to their duties in this House, which are just as great as the duties of men in the trenches at the front.'

The issue came to a head on 21 October, when there was a general discussion in the Committee on the position of the Party. Every speaker took a pessimistic line and the mood of the Committee stalwarts was summed up in a letter which Lord William Scott sent to the Chief Whip that evening:

My dear James,

I am writing this letter in case you get a false impression from the report of your Whip on what I had to say at the '22 Committee today.

I have certain very definite complaints of which the main one is that 1941 was a wasted year. Talk about locusts, no year was more wickedly wasted than 1941, with the result that 1942 was unable to produce a second front.

I complain that instead of 'Blood, and sweat, and tears', we have been given Talk and Talk and Talk.

Throughout the country the Conservative Party has become a cheap joke: the press and the BBC treat us with the contempt that we have earned and deserve.

You yourself are well aware of what the PM thinks of the Tory Rump: he may not say so himself, but R.C., B.B. [Randolph Churchill, Brendan Bracken] and his other satellites are not so careful of their tongues.

You must agree with the fact that as an effective body of opinion either in the House or the Country, the Conservative Party have ceased to exist.

There is no liaison or connection between our 'Leaders' in office and the rank-and-file: the Conservative Whips have become the National Government Whips, and have long ceased to organise and co-ordinate the party, and merely use them as numbers to swell the majority when there is a vote of no confidence.

I am not blaming you personally: you have had a very difficult job, and so far you have been extremely successful. You have a vast amount of work to do, quite apart from looking after the organisation in the House of your principal party: I trust that you will not complain if others fill the gap.

You will make a big mistake if you think that such an organisation is directed against either you or the National Government, though we both realize that some of the more vocal elements in such a set-up are bound to be those who are at present disappointed on personal grounds.

What I do *not* know is whether you personally are aware of the extent or depth of feeling on this matter of most of the quiet Conservative Members, and of our Associations in the country ... the sense of frustration is very acute.

I have sufficient regard for your own personal powers of persuasion to realize that you will be able to make very good use of any success that we may have in our endeavours to restore 'effectiveness' to the rump of the party in the House.

Many members have expressed resentment at the manner in which the 'Chair' treats the Party – I personally think that he has treated us just as we deserve to be treated: we have asked for contempt and we have been accorded it.

The remedy lies in our own hands and I believe that at last after two years we are prepared to apply it.

I only hope that you will look upon the matter in a broad and not unfriendly manner, in time you may even be thankful.

Perhaps you think that we are bound to fail – you may be right in this assumption – we will all in time regret it if we do.

Yours ever,
BILLY.

The Chief Whip sent a conciliatory reply:

My dear Billy,

It is kind of you to have written at such length to let me know what is in your mind.

I realise, of course, that the Party feels that it has lost ground and does not get a fair deal under present conditions – but I think that this is due largely to the existence of an All-Party Government in which, as the largest partner and the most loyal, we have had to give the most. You will, I think, find that there were many similar feelings expressed in the 1917-18 days. As soon as we are able to revert to normal peace-time conditions, the Party would get together again – whether in office or in opposition.

While I will, of course, welcome anything helpful and constructive which will have the effect of consolidating the Party behind, or in support of, the Government, my only anxiety is lest anything should be done to split the Party in the House by forming some sort of separate Parliamentary Party divorcing from it those who are in the Govern-

ment. The formation of an All-Party Government was, I
believe, essential for the country but it is, I admit, detri-
mental to the Party in many ways. At the same time, I hope
that many reasonable and thoughtful people in the country
do give the Party credit for doing what is right in the
National interest. While I, personally, shall remain a
Conservative always, I must under present conditions
continue to serve the Government. I don't think that anyone would disagree with that – but I realise that it may
not benefit me personally in the eyes of some in our Party.
However that can't be helped.

You are quite right in advocating whatever you believe
may be in the best interests of our Party and I shall not,
of course, regard any such action as being in any way
personal.

I only trust that this will not lead to any split – or to
a Party 'divided against itself'. This would weaken us, I
fear, and might take a lot of healing.

Yours ever,

JAMES.

As James Stuart knew, these anxieties about divorcing the
Parliamentary Party from the Government were shared by two
of the most distinguished members of the Committee – Colonel
Walter Eliott and Colonel Oliver Stanley. Walter Eliott, who
had been widely regarded as a potential Prime Minister in
Mr Baldwin's days, was busy reminding members of the split
that had developed in the Conservative Party towards the end
of the Lloyd George coalition. Now he warned his colleagues
that a similar split could develop.

Walter Eliott was listened to with attention but the leading
role at this point was played by Oliver Stanley. Before his
ministerial career had begun in the early 1930s, Oliver Stanley
had claim to be one of the first important parliamentarians to
take the 1922 Committee seriously. In the first months of 1940,
when Winston Churchill had been First Lord of the Admiralty,
Oliver Stanley had been Secretary of State for War, but when
the coalition government had been formed in May 1940, Oliver
Stanley had chosen to go back to the Army.

At the meeting of the Committee on 21 October, 1942, he

had made four telling points: (1) that the supposed bad record of the Party before the War was a millstone round the Party's neck. 'Guilty Men' had done a lot of harm and should be answered; (2) the party didn't know what its policy was. The party had to say what it was aiming to do after the war; (3) the party couldn't regain its place in the House of Commons without reorganisation there, and (4) there had never been such a gulf between members of the party and the leaders.

It was decided that the discussion should be continued at the next meeting. Meanwhile, Oliver Stanley should consult with his colleagues. About a hundred and fifty Members attended the meeting on 18 November. He put forward a seven-point plan for reorganising the Committee and the Party in the House:

(1) A Conservative Party Committee to be formed, of which Ministers and Whips are members as of right.

(2) Only back-benchers eligible to stand as, or vote for the Chairman, Officers and Executive Committee.

(3) Besides meetings of the full committee, there would be meetings confined to the 'unofficial' side. Probably to begin with there would be one full meeting a month.

(4) There would be no sanctions and neither Ministers nor minorities would be bound by the decision of the Committee.
Such decision would however indicate the majority view of the party.

(5) There should be a Conservative Front Bench (say the second bench below the gangway). The Officers, Executive Committee and ex-Ministers would be entitled to sit on it.

(6) The Executive Committee to have the right in all important debates to nominate one speaker representing the majority view of the Committee.

(7) The Executive Committee to be regarded as the 'usual channels' for ascertaining the wishes of the Party.

On 22 November Oliver Stanley was appointed Colonial Secretary in a series of ministerial changes, of which the most important was the departure of Sir Stafford Cripps from the War Cabinet to take over the Ministry of Aircraft Production. Nevertheless, Colonel Stanley attended the Committee by special invitation on 25 November, when the following motion which he had drafted was read:

> That the 1922 Committee appoint a deputation of six Members to discuss with Conservative Ministers, the Chief Whip and the Chairman of the Party the question of re-organization on the lines set out in Colonel Stanley's speech, and report to the Committee.

The resolution was formally moved by Sir Thomas Moore, as Colonel Stanley was no longer eligible to do so. The resolution, as drafted by Colonel Stanley, was carried with six dissentients. The following names, as recommended by the Executive, were approved at the meeting on 2 December: Sir Joseph Nall, Mr Brooke, Wing-Commander James, Squadron-Leader Keeling, Mr Summers and Mr Willink. (Squadron-Leader Keeling was called overseas at short notice, and was replaced by Captain Crowder.)

It was not until the New Year, 27 January, 1943, that Sir Joseph Nall sent to the Executive Committee a draft report of the meeting of the six Members with the Prime Minister, Sir Kingsley Wood and Mr Anthony Eden. The text reads:

> The Prime Minister accompanied by other Ministers discussed the proposals in detail with your sub-committee, and welcomed the suggestion that all members of the Party in the House of Commons, irrespective of whether they hold office or appointment, should be eligible to be members of the Committee, and he agreed that Ministers should take no part in electing the Officers of the Committee. He recognised that it was undesirable for Members of the Government to be elected to office on the Committee or to take part in elections. At the same time, he thought it would be invidious to have rules laid down to prevent this. It was a matter better dealt with by convention than rule, and it would be simple for the Leader of the Party to see that such a convention was adhered to.
>
> The suggestion that the Committee should, on occasion, hold meetings only of Private Members, from which Ministers would be particularly excluded, is not acceptable to the Leader of the Party and it was suggested that when

such occasions arise the Private Members concerned should convene such *ad hoc* meetings as may seem fit to them.

The suggestion that a Conservative Front Bench should be formed below the Gangway was regarded as impracticable and likely to create difficulties which would be unavoidable.

The Leader of the Party, however, thought that the other proposals regarding business in the House, the calling of speakers in debate and communication through the usual channels could, with advantage, be further considered in consultation with the Chief Whip, and the Leader expressed his willingness to further discuss these matters with your sub-committee and the Chief Whip.

It would seem that the whole question may now be divided into two parts, the first being that of the constitution of the Committee in regard to which it would be competent for the Commitee to consider, and, if thought fit, resolve that the name of the Committee be changed to 'The Conservative Members Committee', and that all Members of the Conservative and Unionist Party in the House of Commons, irrespective of the holding of any office or appointment under the Crown, be eligible to be members of the Committee.

On the second part of the question, your sub-committee would like to know that it has the authority of the whole Committee to pursue these other questions outstanding with the Chief Whip and the Leader of the Party.

JOSEPH NALL

From this followed a resolution put to the Committee on 24 February:

(1) That all Members of the Conservative and Unionist Party elected to the House of Commons, irrespective of the holding of office or appointment under the Crown, be eligible to be members of the Committee provided they are in receipt of the Party Whip.

(2) That the name of the Committee be changed to 'The Conservative Members Committee'.

The resolution was moved by Sir Joseph Nall and seconded by

Mr Willink. After a general discussion, and the insertion of 'Unionist' into the proposed new title of the Committee, Sir Joseph Nall's motion was carried by 61 votes to 41, on a second vote only six Members opposed the change in the Committee's name.

When the Committee met on 17 March, the new dispensation was already operating, and four Ministers were present among the 130 Members. But there were still some constitutional loose ends to be tidied up. A question was raised about the position of Mr David Lipson, a widely-respected Independent Conservative whose membership of the Committee had been approved by the Executive in 1939. He had since been a regular attender, but did not possess the password of admission to the newly-constituted Committee – receipt of the Whip. And there were a handful of others, some *persona grata* and some not, who bore either an Independent Conservative or a National Government label. Where did they stand? The judgment was left to the Chief Whip, who ruled that the sole test of membership of the Committee must be that the individual concerned took the Party Whip. Mr Lipson was felt to be a special case, but after some discussion of his claim, it was proposed by Mr Duff Cooper, and agreed, that the matter should be left in the hands of the Executive. Their eventual ruling was to abide by the test of eligibility laid down by the Chief Whip. This was later embodied in a memorandum, duly placed in the Minute Book. It reads:

The recognised test of an MPs political allegiance in the House of Commons is his receipt of a Party Whip.

When, however, a Party is in office, whether entirely responsible for the government of the country, or as a partner in a Coalition Government, the term Party Whip requires interpretation.

In these circumstances the Chief Whip of the Party becomes Parliamentary Secretary to the Treasury and the Whip which he issues is the Government Whip as well as the Party Whip. (There would be no point in issuing two identical whips, one described as the Government Whip and one as the Party Whip.)

So far as the Conservative Party is concerned, a further test of political allegiance would be the eligibility of a

Member to attend a Party meeting. The list of names of such Members is contained in the printed Party Lists which are kept in the Whips' Office.

It is not unusual for Conservatives or Unionists at elections to describe themselves as National Government or National, although they are Conservatives or Unionists and have been properly adopted by the local Associations. It is suggested that the reference books are not a reliable guide as to Party designations and that the authentic lists are those kept by the Whips.

It is plain that the Chief Whip, James Stuart, had many reservations about the proposed reforms, but it is equally plain that the change of title brought a change of tone to the Committee's proceedings. From then on, the 1922 Committee did, in practice, devote much more time to a substantial discussion and criticism of the forthcoming business and the Government's performance in the past weeks.

These contemporary records of meetings held in 1944 give a fair picture of the Committee's deliberations:

On 15 March, 1944, it was noted that

Herbert Williams suggested that any member who cared should subscribe to a leaving presentation to Mr Scott Lindsay, Secretary to the Parliamentary Labour Party. Subscriptions should not exceed 5/-.

Crowder raised the point that in his opinion the duties of Leader of the House and Foreign Secretary were too much for a single individual to hold. Oliver Simmonds agreed, except he said he did not want to see another Stafford Cripps as Leader. Guy Lloyd voiced his anxiety as regards Foreign affairs and wanted Mr Eden to come to the Committee and hear members' views. His anxieties were under two heads (a) too abject an appeasement of Russia; (b) too little regard for the rights of small countries. These views were supported by Loftus, Petherick, Cobb, Alan Graham, Dunglass, Rayner, Manningham-Buller, Murray Sueter and Savory.

Erskine-Hill pointed out that J. Llewellin was due to address the Committee next week and it was difficult to put him off as he had already been put off once. At which someone called out 'Put him off again', and it was agreed the Chairman should ask Mr Eden to come next week when members should make 3-minute statements of their points of criticism and the Secretary of State should reply at the end.

On 21 June, 1944, the Minutes record:

Quintin Hogg pointed out, in connection with the Parliamentary Electors Bill, that it only referred to civilians – 'communists and sea-lawyers'. If there were to be no mention of the forces he might be obliged to move a reasoned motion for rejection.

Cobb asked for plenty of time for Members to study the Town and Country White Paper and Bill before any concrete measure was submitted.

Peter Macdonald suggested that the promised debate on colonial affairs might take place next Thursday, failing any other decision.

Petherick, Turton, Manningham Buller and others asked particularly that Government amendments to the Milk Bill might appear in good time on the paper, in fact as soon as possible.

Nancy Astor said that in Plymouth and probably therefore all over the country Local Committees were composed of crusted old Tories who were quite out of touch with public opinion.

About 18 speakers took part in a debate on political organization. Topics were Topping must go [Sir Robert Topping was General Director of the Conservative and Unionist Central Office and principal Agent of the Party] and how to reinstate constituency agents. On Tommy Dugdale's suggestion, the '22 Committee Executive agreed to appoint a small advisory committee to consult with Central Office on matters of general importance.

On the 1st November, 1944.

Mr Spencer Summers raised the question of the Board of Trade which he said was a lamentable department and a hindrance rather than a help to trade. A new kind of Board and a new President were wanted.

Nall supported this view but added the Department of Overseas Trade is a partner in crime. It was essential to put back the Department of Overseas Trade to the flourishing condition in which it was left by Rob Hudson.

Clarry also spoke in support. Crowder suggested that the mess was not the result of Dalton's inefficiency, but of a deliberate policy in order to make the working of private enterprise more difficult later on. Eccles agreed, and said that Dalton was surrounded by 'London School of Economics activists and the sweepings of Fleet Street'.

Thorneycroft said there was no party division in this, and that if an amendment to the Address was tabled, the Tory Reform Group would come in on it. Dunglass suggested that an amendment never got rid of a Minister. A deputation to the Prime Minister would be better. After a number of other members had spoken (G. Davies, Higgs, Turton, Beverley Baxter, Cobb, Cary, who specifically excluded Charles Waterhouse from the general condemnation) the Chairman [Erskine-Hill] said that though he could not go to the Prime Minister asking for the dismissal of a Socialist and a Liberal Minister, he would do so on the grounds of the general state of the Board of Trade administration.

Manningham Buller wanted more Conservative adjournments, as they seemed all to be raised by the other side and received a good deal of publicity.

Savory raised the question of the Union Jack not being flown over the British High Commission's office in Dublin.

At the end of 1944, John Helias Finnie McEwen succeeded Alec Erskine-Hill as Chairman of the 1922 Committee. Jock McEwen, the third Scot – and the second Old Etonian – to lead the Committee had backed into the Chair by an unusual route. Two of the previous chairmen – Hugh O'Neill and 'Shakes' Morrison – had left the Committee to become Ministers, while a number of the founder members of the Executive had become Whips; but before he became Chairman Jock McEwen had already been both a Minister and a Whip. Jock McEwen had been elected as Member for Berwick in 1931 after spending some years in the Diplomatic Service. He had been Under-Secretary of State for Scotland in the last year of the Chamber-

lain Government, and had rejoined the Government in 1942 as
a Whip. Up until his election as Chairman, he had regularly
attended the Committee as Whip on duty.

It seemed that the new Chairman and the Chief Whip, James
Stuart, should form a formidable partnership. Both men had
served with distinction in Scottish regiments in the first war.
Both men had unexpected literary talents. Jock McEwen was
the only Chairman of the 1922 Committee in the first fifty years
of its existence to translate François Mauriac.

It was a difficult moment at which to take over the Chairmanship. As the war in Europe moved towards its close, there was
mounting concern about the consequences of the Soviet advance
into Eastern Europe; in particular the effect on Poland was a
central issue which came to a head with the Yalta Conference.
A contemporary record of the meeting on 14 February, 1945,
after the Yalta Conference, records the following:

Raikes said it was wrong that the Provisional Government
in Poland should be recognised. The Polish Communist
Government in Lublin had been accepted without consultation with the Polish Government in London, or discussion
in Parliament. Poland had been utterly sold out.

Southby supported, said it was betrayal of the honour
of this country and was bitterly opposed by electors in
this country.

Dunglass said this was a breach of the Atlantic Charter.
A substantial proportion of London Government should
have been included. There must be International supervision of the election in Poland.

Summers said we were giving way to Russia and America
instead of standing up to our principles.

Sidney supported this view.

Petherick also much opposed, said that this was abject
surrender.

Cobb said our national honour involved, should come out
with very little credit.

Willoughby de Eresby, speaking from his Army experience said soldiers were fighting for independent Poland
and not one dictated by Russia.

Donner took same view.

Hamilton Kerr, Lamb, Tree and Hinchingbrooke wished to hear what the Foreign Secretary had to say.

No doubt that the great majority of the Committee were opposed to the present settlement and would speak against it in the House.

The discussion was resumed on the following week.

Naturally most questions or remarks dealt with the Polish question. Loftus, Petherick and Nall said it was a mistake to have a division at all and asked that the question of a Vote of Confidence be reconsidered. Southby asked that representations should be made for a 3-day debate. Manningham-Buller hoped that personal remarks about Stalin would not be made during the debate, as this would not help Anglo-Russian relations. Hogg said the Government is committed to the Crimea Conference and we must support it. The Chairman (McEwen) said the Prime Minister had told him that, as he depended on votes and votes alone, he must know how he stands; that Members must do as they think fit, etc., etc. This was a question on which people felt deeply and must act accordingly; he hoped there would be no recriminations.

N.B. It seemed that the atmosphere on the Polish question was less hectic. No doubt the same division of opinion exists, but Members are more disposed to face realities and the atmosphere generally was easier. An amendment to the Motion will, however, be put down.

Along with concern about the fate of Eastern Europe, the Committee was constantly concerned with the problem of ensuring that those who had served in the Forces were at least as well-placed after demobilisation as those who had stayed in civilian life. Thus, on 1 March, 1945, Lord Woolton, the Minister of Post-War Reconstruction, met a small delegation from the 1922 Committee, to discuss the question of loans to small traders who had served in the Forces. A contemporary record shows that the following points were raised:

1. Loan to the returning soldiers to be raised from £150 to £500.

Lord Woolton replied – danger of inflation and did they really want the State to provide money on this scale, presumably to people who were not credit-worthy? The idea of the £150 was to give a start on the strength of which Banks would give further loans in suitable cases.

2. Request for loan to be to all ex-Servicemen – not merely to men who had had a business before – and disabled men.

Did the deputation mean that every ex-soldier who had, for example, been a shop assistant, or anything else, should be lent money to start a small shop or business? The deputation did not press the point.

3. When were the loans to begin?
Date not yet settled.

4. Will loans be available to men already discharged?
Yes.

5. Can the money be used to purchase an existing business?
Yes.

6. Can something be done to stop 'large stores' (multiple shops, Co-ops, etc.) buying up small businesses?
(Lord Woolton) – Did they really want control to this extent – and to prevent a small man selling his business to anyone he might want to? Deputation on the whole thought not.

But the issue which dominated political discussion towards the end of the European war was the timing of the General Election. Ten years had passed since the last General Election and it was plain that the pressure for an early poll would be considerable. On 11 April, Commander Peter Agnew opened a discussion in the Committee by arguing that a General Election should be held as soon as possible, otherwise propaganda against the Prime Minister as a peace-time prime minister would spread.

Factories would be closing down. The Housing position would get worse. Bull amused the Committee by saying that an old Register, candidates fresh from battlefields (even if they knew little) and lack of Agents were arguments in favour of early Election! Baxter said we should break up the Government and make a Conservative Government – 'to hell with men-of-good-will, etc.'.

The arguments deployed against an early election were:

The necessary delay of machinery (3 weeks notice of Election by the King, etc.), also 25 constituencies have still to be created. The harvest. Difficult to consult agriculture workers, as they are busy during the next few months. There are no Agents. What state is the present Register in? We must not give the impression we are pushing the Liberal-Labour Parties out. Many constituencies still have no candidates. Early election will not give time for Associations to be set up or Service candidates to learn their job, etc., etc.

The Committee, it was recorded, split 60-40 in favour of an early election.

On 8 May the surrender of Germany was announced. On 18 May, Winston Churchill wrote to Clement Attlee, the leader of the Labour Party:

From the talks I have had with you and your principal Labour colleagues I have gathered the impression that the Labour Party, instead of leaving the Government on the defeat of Germany, would be willing to continue in Coalition until the autumn.

I have given the most careful and anxious thought to this suggestion, and I regret to say that in its present form I cannot feel it would be in the public interest. A union of parties like that which now exists should come together and work together, not for particular date without regard to world event, but for the achievement of some great national purpose transcending all party differences ...

I therefore make you the following proposal, which I earnestly hope you will not readily reject – namely, that we should fix upon another object for our joint endeavours and adjourn the question of our separation until it is gained ... It would give me great relief if you and your friends were found resolved to carry on with us until a decisive victory has been gained over Japan ...

I am conscious, however, in the highest degree of our duty to strengthen ourselves by a direct expression of the nation's will. If you should decide to stand on with us, all united together until the Japanese surrender is compelled, let us discuss means of taking the nation's opinion; for example, a referendum on the issue whether in these conditions the life of this Parliament should be further prolonged.

Clement Attlee's reply was brusque. On 23 May the Coalition was dissolved, and the Conservative caretaker government was formed.

On 30 May, the Committee met, for the first time in five years, under an exclusively Conservative Government; and a ragbag of minor party points were discussed once the Chief Whip had outlined the probable course of business before the dissolution of Parliament on 15 June. Sir Wavell Wakefield wanted to know if party candidates were expected to display the same colours, or would it be left to individual choice? Sir Frank Sanderson wanted to know about names. Could individual members decide whether to call themselves Conservative, National Conservative, or plain National candidates? Sir Arnold Gridley wanted to know about dates for posting election addresses to the Forces.

On 12 June, the 1922 Committee met for the last time in the 1935-45 Parliament. The subject under discussion was a familiar one – the damage done to the party by Lord Beaverbrook's speeches. The majority view seemed to be that on the whole, the *Daily Express* did more good than Beaverbrook did harm.

The Committee, then, did not end this important phase of its life with a bang or even a fanfare, but during the coalition days it had a record that it could be proud of. The Officers and the Executive had rarely tried to challenge the Government's handling of affairs, but it had provided both a safety valve and a forum in which party controversies could be thrashed out. In the Lloyd George coalition, many Conservative leaders had wholly lost touch with the rank and file of the Parliamentary party. The fact that this did not happen in the Churchill coalition was in some small part due to meetings of the 1922 Committee. At a time when Ministers had little time to think of party matters, the Committee had always provided a secure base where issues could be examined from an avowedly partisan viewpoint. This did not seem to matter much in May 1940. It mattered a very great deal in May 1945.

On 5 July, the country voted. Because of the difficulty of collecting the votes of servicemen overseas, the result was not announced until 26 July, 1945. The size of the swing came as a shock to most Members. One Commonwealth candidate was elected; 2 Irish Nationalists; 2 Communists; 3 Independent Labour Party Members; 9 Ulster Unionists; 12 Liberals; 13 National Liberals; 14 Independents; 189 Conservatives and 392 Labour Party Members. The old 1922 Committee had been destroyed.

6

This Pleasing Assembly
(1945-51)

WHEN THE COMMITTEE MET in October 1945 to elect a new Chairman and Executive, Lord John Hope, one of the new Members, had the temerity to ask that the actual election should be delayed for a week 'in order that they might be able to inform themselves of the suitability of the various candidates. After a long discussion, it was decided to adopt this procedure.'

This plea and its acceptance was a measure of the casualty rate in the ranks of the old 1922 Committee. Not only had half of the seats held by the Conservative Party been lost, but nearly half the seats that had been retained were now filled by new men. Sir Reginald Clarry, the last of the founding fathers, had been beaten at Newport, and the two immediate past Chairmen – Alec Erskine-Hill and Jock McEwen – were also defeated.

When the election was held, the new Chairman was Sir Arnold Gridley, who described himself in a contemporary entry in *Who's Who* as 'For many years engaged in the administration of various Electric Supply and Manufacturing Undertakings at home and overseas; during European War was Controller of Electric Power Supply at the Ministry of Munitions and Chairman of various War Cabinet sub-committees'. He has been described by various of his successors as 'wise', 'cautious', 'sensible', and 'a warm tea-cosy of a man'. He had been brought up in Bristol, where he went to Bristol Grammar School, and was elected Member for Stockport in 1935.

But even with so many new faces in the ranks, there was a quick reversion to familiar themes. At the meeting which elected Sir Arnold to the Chair, Beverley Baxter was on his feet attacking Sir John Anderson for lack of vigour in leading the opposition to the Bank of England Bill. Doubts were then expressed about the effectiveness of the Scrutiny Committee –

a Shadow Cabinet sub-committee which allocated Bills to the appropriate specialist party committees and appointed a Shadow Minister to take charge of the opposition to the Bill in the House.

This was followed by a request that another committee should be set up to act as a link between back-benchers and Central Office, and once again there was a suggestion that there should be a special committee for new members. This was set up under the avuncular Chairmanship of Major Guy Lloyd, who arranged for the new Members to meet together on several occasions, when they were briefed on procedure by such experienced parliamentarians as Harry Crookshank.

In fact, the meetings of the 1922 Committee provided plenty of procedural education for new members as, week after week, the tactics for the following week were discussed in some detail. Generally the loudest voices were raised in favour of all-out opposition on all fronts all the time, and even in the first discouraging months of the new Parliament, it was rarely necessary for the Whips to call for a better attendance. But on Fridays there was usually a thin House, as Members left for their constituencies. Thus, it is recorded that on Thursday, 14 February, 1946, the Whip on duty was authorised to deliver a mild reprimand:

> While the attendance has been very good on other days, I must draw attention to the importance of attendance on Fridays by all who can arrange to be present in the House.
>
> Last Friday, we were anxious to have a division on the Ministers of the Crown Bill, due to the fact that the Government had not done anything to meet us in spite of their promise to consider one or two points during committee stage. Owing to the very small attendance, it would have created a very bad impression if we had publicised our weakness. The press would certainly have commented upon it.

But what was the point of it all? What general tactics should the Opposition adopt? Was it right to try and hold up the Labour Government's legislative programme for as long as possible? When Charles Taylor raised these questions, Captain Harry Crookshank, who was already establishing a reputation

as the Party's leading tactical expert in the House, was ready
to reply – intelligence and teamwork were all important. Weaker
Ministers should be exposed and deficiencies in administration
should be probed. Where it lay in the Opposition's hands, business should be arranged to cause the Government the maximum
inconvenience, but where Ministers were strong and competent,
the best weapon in debate was silence, or idle chatter.

It was comparatively rare for the discussion to move from
the tactical level to the strategic, as on 1 August, 1946, when
a discussion on transport policy was opened by Peter Thorneycroft. Some leaders of the road haulage industry had produced
a scheme which accepted a wide measure of control from Whitehall, in return for retention of private ownership and
the continued existence of the C. licence system, which
allowed traders to carry their own goods. Peter Thorneycroft
had urged the Committee to back the road haulage plan and
David Gammans had gone even further by arguing that the
case against outright nationalisation would be strengthened by
having an alternative scheme to discuss. Oliver Poole, a future
Chairman of the Party, disagreed; the scheme was too mono-
polistic to merit support. The most scathing comment came from
David Eccles, who asserted that the Conservative Party had no
industrial policy or principles. As soon as Parliament reassembled
after the summer recess, Anthony Eden, the Deputy Leader,
came to the Committee to announce the establishment of a policy
committee to go into the question of formulating an industrial
policy – an announcement which provoked a demand that agricultural policy should not be overlooked. Just over six months
later, the 1922 Committee discussed the Industrial Charter –
the product of the policy committee's urgent deliberations. Sir
Waldron Smithers thought that this was a wishy-washy document
and a compromise with Socialism. But Sir Waldron, not for the
first or last time, was alone in his demand for a more dogmatic
renunciation of pseudo-socialism.

Meanwhile, the mood of the Party and the country had
changed between the establishment of the policy committee
and the publication of the Industrial Charter. When the Industrial Policy Committee was set up in October 1946, the Labour
Government seemed invulnerable in the House and in the
country. By the time the Industrial Charter was published, the

breakdown of fuel supplies in the winter of 1946-47, coupled with the prospect of continued austerity and a belief that the economy was being mismanaged, had done substantial damage both to the country's confidence in a Labour Government and the labour movement's confidence in itself.

This new mood was reflected in Mr Churchill's speech of thanks to the Committee for its effective opposition made at the last meeting before the summer recess in 1947. A contemporary record notes the following Churchillian points:

(a) No Coalition – this would be robbing the country of an effective alternative Government.

(b) We should not say too much about what we will do when we get power – 'it is dangerous to prescribe until you are called in'.

(c) As the Party grows stronger, the country is getting weaker. We should be careful not to show any 'satisfaction' about this – but show ourselves willing to do all we can to help the national cause.

(d) We must make no promises we cannot fulfil in due course.

(e) We must not desert the Industrial Charter, which is a most valuable document.

In those post-war years, public opinion polls were not yet regarded as a foolproof guide to the electorate's inclination and correspondingly greater significance was attached to by-election results.

In all the contested seats at the General Election of 1945, the Labour Party and its allies had captured 48.2% of the total vote, the Conservatives and their allies had received 39.9% and the other parties plus Independents another 11.9%. As an exact science psephology was in its infancy in the late 1940s, but it did not require much expertise to establish that a swing of 4.2% from Labour to Tory would produce an almost exact dead heat. In 1947, Labour's poll at the by-elections showed a loss of 6.5% while the Conservatives were gaining 7.2%. 1948 proved to be an even better year for the Conservative Party with a Labour loss of 7.7% and a Conservative gain of 8.2%. But although some of the swings at individual by-elections had been exceptionally large, no 'ordinary' Labour seat had been captured by a Conservative up until the end of 1948.

Early in 1949, a by-election at South Hammersmith looked like providing a victory to set the Conservative Party on the road to victory at the General Election, which could not be postponed beyond the summer of 1950. South Hammersmith had recorded substantial Conservative majorities in the 1930s, but in 1945 a Labour candidate, W. T. Adams, had received 12,502 votes against the 9,044 for the sitting Conservative Member, Sir Douglas Cooke.

South Hammersmith went to the polls on 23 February, 1949, the day on which the French Cabinet discussed a draft agreement for Vietnamese independence. The British electorate, however, could be expected to take greater interest in the prediction of Professor G. A. Scott-Watson, the Chief Agricultural Adviser to the Ministry of Agriculture, that bread rationing might be in force in 1952 if American aid were not continued. Meanwhile, the report of the Lynskey Tribunal into allegations of corruption at the Board of Trade had not helped to get the Labour campaign off to a swinging start. All this encouraged the Conservative Party campaign managers to persuade Mr Churchill to make a triumphal tour of the constituency on the eve of poll, in support of their energetic candidate, Anthony Fell.

The result was a minor fiasco. The Labour poll actually rose by more than two and a half thousand votes, to 15,223. Anthony Fell increased the Conservative vote by more than four and a half thousand votes to 13,610, but the Labour majority was still 1,613 votes. As the *Economist* noted in a leading article:

It is not surprising, therefore, that a smile of demure satisfaction should have been visible upon the faces of the Labour Party managers. If, at the beginning of their last year of office, and despite the many restrictions of personal freedom that are still in force, the Government can win a marginal constituency and thus maintain unbroken their record of victory at the by-elections, they can argue that the confidence of the electorate is still in their keeping ...

Elections are verdicts pronounced for or against the government of the day, and every opposition always seems negative and helpless to do anything but reap such harvest of discontent as comes up. There are dangers for a party in having too cut-and-dried a policy while in opposition. But a party must stand for something; if it has not precise policy it should have principles; and the electorate's judgement is greatly influenced by the skill and sincerity with which the Opposition presents the case against the Government. It is here that the Conservatives have shown themselves to be woefully deficient.

It is possible to isolate two particular causes of their failure as an opposition. In the first place, the Conservative Party has been so anxious to avoid the odium of opposing the social policies of the present government that they have jettisoned most of the logical grounds for criticising its economic policy ... Instead of standing forth as the champions of wise and vigorous government, they have allowed themselves, by talking in generalities about abstract principles such as 'freedom' and 'enterprise', to be represented as the captious remnant of a bygone social order.

In the second place, they have treated the rise of Socialism as an aberration from the normal British way of life, instead of recognising that the Socialist ideal of the welfare state is very closely in tune with the ideas of a frustrated and war-weary nation ... The Conservatives have over the past three and a half years confounded jibes against the Socialist Government with the presentation of an alternative policy.

For both these defects, Mr Churchill must take a heavy personal share of the blame. He was a very great war leader. He still is a world statesman – as witness the way in which his Fulton speech, so much derided at the time it was made three years ago, has become the accepted policy of the western world. But the leader of a party has also to inspire his followers on matters of domestic policy. It is perhaps to his credit that Mr Churchill is such an imperfect party leader. But that he is not giving his party the leadership it requires is hardly any longer open to doubt. His willingness to commit his colleagues to impossible political situations without participating in the ensuing battle partly accounts for the many humiliating defeats which have been inflicted on the Opposition. His unwillingness to engage in hard thought about the future – save on the plane of international policy – has stultified the growth of a coherent body of policy and criticism ... His magnificent oratorical powers are accompanied by a love of generalities at a time when the Conservative leaders need above all to be crisp and incisive.

The South Hammersmith by-election in fact produced the most severe crisis of confidence in Mr Churchill's leadership since the defeat of 1945. On Thursday, 3 March, 1949, Mr Churchill attended a crowded meeting of the 1922 Committee to listen to the post-mortem discussion.

Robin Turton opened with a vigorous attack on the deployment of the Front Bench and was particularly scathing on the handling of the recent debate on the substantial supplementary estimate for the brand-new Health Service.

Many others supported and embellished this theme, but perhaps the most vigorous attack on the current Conservative strategy came from Quintin Hogg who, according to one contemporary record argued:

General effect of Conservative propaganda – snarling and whining at enemy.

Not enough positive idealism.

Majority of Party taking too gloomy view of economic future:

If we cry wolf too often and disasters after end of Marshall Aid do not come, result disastrous to us.

Reaction of people to disaster would not be towards Conservatives, but towards greater controls.

After more than an hour of unprecedented bluntness from the floor, Mr Churchill rose to reply. The same record noted these points:

Fundamental dilemma was – should we present, regardless of popularity, dark facts confronting us, e.g.:

Living on American aid – Government squandering – taxation ruinous.

Query – Better to lose Election than be responsible for

encouraging false hopes? Then we could say, we told you so.

If Socialists get second lease of life, evils will be grievous.

Mr Churchill *will not* give candidates idea we shall lose.

Do not damn food subsidies, but stress bad bulk buying, etc.

Do not call halt in Social reforms – fatal.

Impossible to give clear-cut rulings on all questions.

Why wave of pessimism? Mr Churchill does not feel it. Do not be cowed because of a bump here and there.

Tendencies show that Socialists will suffer heavy defeats at Election.

Management in House of Commons – Mr Churchill does not give whole time, but Mr Eden has given great satisfaction. In his absence, rely on Mr Stanley (applause).

Consultative Committee to meet weekly.

Electors do not watch House of Commons from day to day.

Mr Churchill does not think tendencies *against* us.

Socialists expected worse results; therefore, correspondingly elated because results not so bad.

Mr Churchill thinks Socialists will hold on till last minute for Election.

Time for re-statement of leading points in our policy and position?

In consultation Mr Churchill will shape statement to be made soon.

Would deprecate brutalising the position by sweeping away Social Welfare policy – feel our way.

Not new programme – *re*-statement of Party policy.

Mr Churchill proposes this autumn to 'clear his own personal decks'; concentrate on electioneering side.

Will not change system in House of Commons. Mr Eden back soon; Mr Churchill's visit to US may be of import in future. Then throw energies into coming Election.

Not down-hearted.

Solid core of Socialist strength exists, *but* figures show continued growth of *our* strength.

The agreed statement issued after the two-hour meeting hardly captured the flavour of the meeting:

At the weekly meeting of the Conservative Members' Committee the lessons of the South Hammersmith Election were the subject of full and frank discussion, in which Mr Churchill took part.

It was agreed that the result of the Election in no way contradicted the trend of the electorate towards the principles of the Conservative Party; that the organisation under Lord Woolton had worked excellently, and that there was no cause for discouragement in the fact that the Party had not recovered the seat.

The 1922 Committee had shown that it was prepared to bark at Mr Churchill in his presence, but the great majority of Members had no desire to bite or to seek to force an early retirement of their Leader. At this time, Mr Churchill seems to have kept a wary eye open for any move within the 1922 Committee to seek a replacement 'because of my advanced age', but a majority of the Committee's Executive seem to have shared in full measure their Leader's reluctance to get involved in too many detailed policy statements.

It is plain that Mr Churchill took considerable trouble with his preparations for his regular meetings with the full 1922 Committee or its Executive; but there were also to be some surprising moments – such as the time when Mr Churchill interrupted the Chairman, Sir Arnold Gridley, with the words 'And pray, Sir Arnold, how did you come to constitute yourselves into this pleasing assembly?'

At the time of the Committee's formation, Sir Winston, of course, had not been a Conservative, and in view of Sir Winston's Liberal and Independent interludes it is not altogether surprising that, during the post-war period of Opposition, Sir Winston should have been particularly anxious to ensure that Liberals and Conservatives joined forces to fight the Labour Government, indeed considerable efforts were made to explore the possibility of liaison, or even fusion, with the Liberal Party. At the beginning of the 1947-48 session the National Liberal Members had been invited to join the Committee.

As Sir Harry Legge-Bourke recalls:
Considerable attempts were therefore made to explore the possibilities of joining up with the Liberals. One private dinner-party took place in the early years of the 1945-50 Parliament at the National Liberal Club with this particular aim in view, and a selection of senior and junior Members of the Parliamentary Party attended a dinner there together with the Liberals in the House of Commons, and leading members of the London Liberal Party. The discussions could certainly not be regarded as a rapprochement, although I noticed with amusement that, hanging on the wall was a picture of my own maternal grandfather, who had been Campbell-Bannerman's Minister of Agriculture. Could it ever be that the Liberals could abandon the agricultural policy expressed in their famous Land Song which that same grandfather had once sung in the House of Lords? 'The Land, the Land, the Land on which we stand ... God gave the Land to the people' seemed all too similar to nationalisation which was then very much part of the longer-term agricultural policy of the Labour Party.

So when in due course the 1922 Committee – with Sir Winston himself present – came to discuss this matter, the auspices were not entirely propitious. It was Peter Thorneycroft who was put up to propound the case for changing the Party's name in order to make it easier for the Liberals to come together and join in the fight against Socialism; but, brilliantly though he presented his case, it was not long before a yet more effective pulverisation of it was delivered by Harry Strauss and Quintin Hogg to the general approval of the Party. So the meeting broke up, with Sir Winston not entirely delighted with the outcome. After the tension generated by the South Hammersmith by-election, the Committee quickly and characteristically turned to more domestic matters. The new Debating Chamber which replaced the one destroyed on the night of 10 May, 1941, was rapidly nearing completion and the Committee was properly concerned with the shape and colour and spacing of the back-benches.

The Committee's criticism of the plans seems to have been accepted and the result certainly gave widespread satisfaction.

Meanwhile, the lingering disappointment of South Hammersmith was brushed aside by the imminent prospect of more elections. On the week after the South Hammersmith inquest Central Office was busy asking for help from the back-benches in the Local Government elections which were just about to begin.

Some exception was taken to the form of the request, but relations between the Committee and the rest of the Party Organisation were soon to be formalised by the adoption of the Maxwell-Fyfe Report on party organisation. The 1922 Committee Executive had four places reserved on the Executive Committee of the Party's National Union – a body with close to two hundred members. It was also to have four seats on the important and smaller policy committee. But the most eye-catching policy formulation in the autumn of 1949 had been performed by the Party Conference itself. Egged on by a fiery speech from Miss Patricia Hornsby-Smith, the Conference had pledged the Party to build 300,000 houses a year.

At its first meeting after the Conference, the Committee discussed this pledge, and Ernest Marples gave an optimistic report:

> He said that in his opinion it was possible to build 300,000 a year after a short time under certain conditions. He thought that within 5 years this could be achieved at a reasonable price.
>
> He wanted a Housing Debate to convince Socialist back-benchers that it could be done, as many of them, including Stokes, did not agree with Bevan.
>
> The point was that efficiency was 25% below pre-war. Payment by results could alter this. The Ministry of Works experiments had already proved this. This would add between 20,000 and 30,000 houses. The question of smaller houses would add a further considerable number. America is today satisfied with a smaller house than we are building. Then certain amenities could be cut; there is already precedent for this in the reduction of certain

specifications in school buildings. If the problem was tackled on these lines he believed about 130,000 extra new houses could be built. His views were well received by the Meeting.

It was not altogether surprising that the discussions of the Committee should have been increasingly dominated by thoughts of the election.

On 8 December, 1949, when he came to the 1922 Committee to give his 'end of term' speech, Mr Churchill reminded the Committee that the Whips had not been over-fussy about attendance except for the most important divisions, and that the years since 1945 had been an interlude during which Members could have some licence to broaden their outlook and experience outside the House 'but that of course if we come back next time with a small majority or in a narrow minority, Members would have to be prepared for a very much stricter interpretation of the Whips duties'.

By the time that the Committee reassembled, Mr Churchill's oblique prophecy of narrow majorities had been wholly justified. On Thursday, 23 February, exactly one year after the Hammersmith by-election, the country went to the polls. The first returns from the cities and towns suggested that the Labour Party had retained the confidence of the electorate, but as the results from the country districts came in on Friday, the gap narrowed. 12,502,567 votes had elected 298 Conservative and Unionist MPs, and two more had been returned unopposed; 2,621,548 Liberal votes had won them 9 seats; while 13,266,592 Labour votes had won 315 seats. Three Independents had also been elected, so the Labour Government held on to office by the skin of its teeth.

The hairs-breadth majority gained by the Labour Government drastically altered the whole nature of the tactical discussions which absorbed so much of the 1922 Committee's time. From 1945 to 1950, these arguments were of largely academic interest. At the best, vigorous opposition might win some concessions. A clause here and a clause there might be altered to meet the wishes of the Party, but there was no hope of defeating the Government on the floor of the House unless some major split developed in the Government's own ranks. Delay rather than defeat had become the prime objective. But now it was clear that the Labour Government was vulnerable on the floor of the House. If the pressure were sufficiently stern and unrelenting, the Government might even be driven from office.

Meanwhile, the composition of the Committee had been drastically altered by the election. Once again, nearly half the Members were new to parliamentary ways – and once again, there were calls for a separate committee for new Members. For the first five weeks of the new session the Whips announcement of forthcoming business often included some notes of special guidance to the younger members.

It was inevitable that the influx of new recruits should weaken the more informal club-like atmosphere that had developed in the post-war years. With so few Members, the gap between the party leaders and the back-benchers had tended to diminish. Everyone had been in the same boat and it had been rather a small boat. It is inevitable that any record of the Committee's activities should dwell on criticism of the leadership. At times of adversity the Committee is a place for letting off steam. Thus an accurate record of the Committee's proceedings will inevitably accentuate the negative. This is particularly true of the period from 1945-50 when, by many accounts, there was an exceptional spirit of cameraderie and mutual respect within the Parliamentary Party. It is a pity that the surviving records of the Committee during this period are particularly inadequate.

Fortuitously, the enlargement of the Committee coincided with the election, on 30 March, 1950, of a particularly strong Executive Committee under the continuing chairmanship of Sir Arnold Gridley.

No less than six of the Executive Committee – John Boyd-Carpenter, David Eccles, Freddy Erroll, Selwyn Lloyd, Peter Thorneycroft and Derek Walker-Smith – were all to become members of the Cabinet or to be given major departmental responsibilities within ten years.

Two more Committee members – Henry Strauss and David Gammans – soon became Junior Ministers. One of the Vice-Chairmen, Robin Turton, became Minister of Health, and the two Secretaries, Alan Noble and Gerald Wills, were soon recruited to the Foreign Office and the Whips Office respectively. When the normal 1922 elections were held at the beginning of the next session, the political bite of this group was reinforced by the election of Nigel Birch, Kenneth Pickthorn and John Vaughan Morgan. Even in a party with talent to spare it was a notable Committee.

One of the Secretary's first duties was to organise a dinner for Mr Churchill to mark the Golden Jubilee of his first election to the House of Commons, and a considerable effort was made to gather together all his old parliamentary colleagues.

On 31 October, some 257 colleagues sat down at the Savoy to a menu packed with allusions to his electoral career.

LE DINER

LA TASSE DE TORTUE
au sherry d'Oldham, 1900
Les galettes de Dundee

LE SUPRÊME DE SOLE
de Douvres, Hastings, Sandwich, New Romney, Hythe – et Manchester
aux champignons de la forêt d'Epping

LES PERDREAUX RÔTIS SUR CANAPÉ CLÉMENTINE
L'unique sauce anglaise
Les pommes de terre toujours nouvelles de Woodford
Les petis pois d'un grand ami de la France
La salade mixte des adversaires politiques

LES ANGES À CHEVAL ONZE FOIS GAGNANT

LES POMMES COX'S ORANGE SANS DÉSACCORD

LE CAFÉ HOT AND STRONG À LA W.S.C.

The charge for the dinner was 21/- a head, exclusive of wine – but the members of the 1922 needed substantial quantities of brandy and champagne to fortify themselves for the parliamentary battles ahead. The question of how these battles should be conducted continued to dominate the discussions within the 1922 Committee.

Bob Boothby was, perhaps, the most vehement of those who wanted to keep the Parliamentary temperature at fever-pitch, but he had many supporters. At a tactical discussion opened by John Boyd-Carpenter on 2 November, 1950, Kenneth Pickthorn, the tart-tongued constitutional historian, had argued in favour of abolishing the pairing system in this Parliament. When David Renton bravely put forward the argument that barristers found it difficult to attend in the afternoon and that it was undesirable to have a House of full-time politicians, Victor Raikes made the most ferocious attack on this argument, and suggested that if maximum pressure were combined with a no-pairing rule, up to six by-elections could be forced before the end of the winter. This extreme position did not gain much support and as one Member noted after the discussion, 'There is no doubt they want the best of both worlds – i.e. to beat the Government periodically, to keep them constantly on their toes; and at the same time, to have the maximum amount of individual freedom ... I believe that the majority of Members, provided the Whips are sympathetic, will quite happily support any decision the Leader makes to leave the whole thing fairly fluid.'

But how far in practice could the opposition be pressed? Within one month Beverley Baxter was objecting to the imposition of a three-line Whip while Mr Attlee was in Washington discussing the conduct of the Korean War with President Truman. We must not allow party considerations to affect the national interest, it was argued, while others suggested that the swift removal of Mr Attlee from office was the highest national interest of all.

The broad discussion was still going on when a new young Whip, Mr Edward Heath, came to the Committee. There were a number of special announcements to make. 'Mr Heath stated that the matter of admitting visitors to the Palace of Westminster during the Festival of Britain was still under consideration by the Committee appointed by Mr Speaker.' Fears had been expressed that Members would be overwhelmed with requests by constituents for trips round the palace during the Festival, and the novel suggestion that guides should be allowed to take parties round on weekday mornings had been put forward

as a way of dealing with the expected rush. The Committee
had also been exercised by the vexed question of the opening
of the Festival Fun Fair on Sundays.

'Mr Heath also stated that the Leader supported and commended the suggestion of appointing a select committee on the
admissability of Questions and that the Chief Whip would discuss
the matter further with the Government Chief Whip.' Sir
Herbert Williams had been particularly vigorous in suggesting
that the parliamentary clerks were shielding Ministers unduly
by showing unnecessary zeal in ruling Questions out of order. The
limits of ministerial responsibility when it came to answering·
questions had been a source of argument ever since Parliamentary
Questions began, but the controversy had been exacerbated
under the 1945 Labour Government by the ruling that Questions
could not be asked about the day-to-day administration of the
nationalised industries. This was to remain a bone of contention
for years.

Charles Waterhouse, who had been Parliamentary Secretary
under Hugh Dalton at the Board of Trade for most of the war,
finally opened yet another discussion on tactics. In the past,
Charles Waterhouse had urged a cautious approach. Now he
demanded 'fractious opposition' with no pairing except by
special permission, and more time-wasting. This line was supported by a number of senior back-benchers, but Robin Turton
argued that the country would not understand fractiousness. Bob
Boothby was even more fractious than Charles Waterhouse. He
wanted the House kept up day and night with relays of speakers.
Perhaps the most powerful argument raised in favour of modera-
tion came from James Stuart, the former Chief Whip. He
believed that the days of filibustering were over. It would merely
antagonise the country, and defeats on the Committee Stage of
Bills would not in fact bring the Government down. Beverley
Baxter went on to argue that the recent defence debate had been
mishandled. The public had not understood the vote of censure.
'The Party was winning in the country but losing in the House.
The 1922 Committee was no longer powerful and Members had
become mere lobby fodder.' A rather more optimistic view
was put by Lord Dunglass and Lord John Hope, but some
variations on these themes were raised at almost every meeting
between March and May. On 14 June, Mr Churchill himself

came to listen to Bob Boothby open yet another lengthy analysis of the tactical options.

By no means all the blows aimed at the Labour Government were planned in the 1922 Committee. Inflation was raging. Taxation had been increased. Aneurin Bevan resigned along with Harold Wilson and John Freeman. As recently as February 1950 the 1922 Committee had devoted some time to a discussion of how to deal with Aneurin Bevan in debate. Meanwhile, another shock was struck by the Persian régime of the eccentric Dr Mussadeq, who had nationalised the enormous British oil interests in his country. Many Conservatives were anxious about the lack of effective protest on behalf of the Government by Herbert Morrison, the Foreign Secretary. On 28 June, Lord Dunglass opened a brief discussion attended by Mr Churchill. Lord Dunglass and his colleagues wanted the Party's views made plain as soon as possible. A vote of censure after a decision to evacuate Abadan would be too late, 'if we did not speak out quickly we should be overcome by events'. Mr Churchill 'appealed to Members to wait until next week and asked for their confidence. He said we should not fail in our duty if we showed restraint for a few days.'

The Persian issue was raised again on 12 July by Fitzroy Maclean, when Mr Butler attended. That senior American diplomat Averell Harriman was attempting a mission of conciliation and in view of this trip 'a considerable majority of the Members were in favour of not having a debate'. Two weeks later there was another full-dress debate in the Committee on the Abadan issue. This time there was a near unanimous call for a strong line, with the strongest words coming from Anthony Head and David Ormsby-Gore, who also demanded a firm line with Eygpt over the Sudan issue. This time there were two front-benchers to listen to the Committee – Harold Macmillan and Rab Butler. Their duet closed the last Committee meeting of the session and, as it turned out, the last meeting of the Committee in that spell of opposition.

On Thursday, 25 October, the country went to the polls again. This time the Conservatives and their allies polled 1,200,000 more votes than they had in February 1950, and they won 25 extra seats. The Liberal vote fell by almost 2,000,000 to 730,556, but the number of Liberal seats only slipped from nine to six. The Labour vote actually rose by almost 700,000, to 13,948,605, but the number of seats which they held slipped to 295. After six years and three months, the Conservatives were back in power.

7

Suez to Supermac

(1951-59)

WHEN SIR ARNOLD GRIDLEY first became Chairman of the 1922
Committee in 1945, Labour Members were singing the Red
Flag and proclaiming 'We are the Masters now'. It was perhaps
symbolic that when, after six years in the Chair, Sir Arnold
decided to retire, the last issue he had to deal with as Chairman
was the question whether Members should be advised not to
address the House in dinner-jackets.

After a contest with Colonel Alan Gomme-Duncan and Sir
Leonard Ropner, Derek Walker-Smith was elected Chairman.
A short, determined, eloquent barrister, Derek Walker-Smith
followed in the legal tradition of Erskine-Hill, Spens, Morrison
and Rentoul – he also shared Sir Gervais Rentoul's affection
for Ciceronian oratory. On the literary side, Derek Walker-
Smith's range was even wider than that of Jock McEwan. He
had written a study of divorce and its problems, he had colla-
borated on a play *Bloody Mary* with Giles Playfair, and he was
also the author of *A Critical Annotation of the Royal Institute
of British Architects Standard Form of Building Contract*. In
opposition, he had contributed frequently to the *Daily Express*
and other newspapers; and he had been criticised at one meeting
of the Committee because these articles were sometimes at vari-
ance to the party line.

Colonel Alan Gomme-Duncan, a former Black Watch officer
who had briefly been HM Inspector of Prisons for Scotland,
was one of the Vice-Chairmen along with John Morrison, the
Member for Salisbury, who had suggested at the previous meeting that a party leader should broadcast to the country about
the economic state of the nation 'as we found it when we took
power'.

Nine of the twelve Executive Committee Members elected

in November 1950 had joined the Government and the new Executive Committee elected at the end of November 1951 looked less like a shadow cabinet and more like a group that would take a robustly back-bench view of their Government's performance. Only four of the new Committee were later to hold office – Douglas Dodds Parker, Freddie Erroll, Lord John Hope and Jack Profumo. Lady Davidson, who had been co-opted to the Executive Committee during the war, was elected in her own right while the presence of Sir Will Darling and Lord Hinchingbrooke was an insurance against any lack of forthrightness. Of the 39 candidates for the 12 places on the Executive no less than 8, including Reggie Maudling and Enoch Powell, had first been elected to the House as recently as February 1950. The two chief vote-getters among the new entry were John Vaughan Morgan and Ted Leather, with Reggie Maudling a close third. Derek Walker-Smith has described the new Executive's relations with the new Government:

Although the function of the Committee is more important when the Party is in Office, its position, as a Private Members or Back Bench Committee, vis-à-vis the Front Bench is in fact always stronger and easier when the Party is in Opposition. The reason for this is that Shadow Ministers are not separated from their Back Bench colleagues by the mystique of Office or the realities of power, and dialogue consequently takes place on a more equal footing. This had certainly been true in the 1945 Parliament, where senior Shadow Ministers, such as Oliver Stanley, habitually attended and frequently contributed to the weekly meetings.

This general rule applied with particular force in 1951. The Administration which then took Office under its almost legendary leader was one of great distinction with its fair share of the feeling natural to Governments that Administration is for Ministers and not to be canvassed beyond a reasonable minimum with the rank and file on whose support they rested. On the other hand, of course, the task and main justification of the 1922 Committee is to ensure that Back Bench opinion is brought to bear and taken into account.

So the first problem was to establish the necessary

rapport with the Prime Minister. This may not seem a great
problem, and would not be a great problem no doubt with
the ordinary run of Prime Ministers. But with Mr Churchill,
a formidable, isolated and elevated figure, without at that
time even a PPS to bridge the gulf, it was obviously a
different and more difficult matter. With some kindly help,
however, including that of James Stuart, the problem was
solved, and in the New Year I had my first interview with
the Prime Minister, and a little later took the Officers and
Executive to see him in formal deputation.

The pattern thus set was maintained for the rest of the
Parliament. Sometimes I saw the Prime Minister alone,
normally on his summons, and sometimes he received the
Officers and Executive collectively, generally at my request.
For the formal deputations, I presented an Agenda, pre-
viously prepared in consultation with the Executive. To
this he dutifully had regard, but he allowed himself abundant
and agreeable latitude to leave the scheduled path for
comment on contemporary events and excursions into
history ...

It was, in the event, well for the Government as well as
the Committee that the pattern was established, so as to
maintain close contact between the Government and its
supporters, as within a few months the Government had
run into difficulties. The Committee was disturbed by the
timing and presentation of the Government's actions, and
in March, at his request, I sent the Prime Minister a
memorandum on Government publicity and the presentation of its case.

In fact, the Government's difficulties continued for some
months; and as the time came in June for the Committee's
Annual Lunch to the Prime Minister, the press was carrying stories of disquiet in the Parliamentary Party. Mr
Churchill asked me to see him to talk about the speech that
he was to make at the Lunch. There were at that time
some Members of the Committee who felt that the Prime
Minister, who after all was 77, should go; but on his asking
me as to the strength of this feeling, I was able to assure
him that it was very much a minority view.

In the event, the Lunch went off well, and the Prime

Minister's speech was very favourably received. By the autumn the Government's stock was higher, and the subjects under discussion, though diverse, were not difficult.

The first issue of importance that the Committee had discussed when it met after the 1951 General Election was the future of the BBC. In 1949 the Labour Government had set up a powerful Committee under Lord Beveridge to review the position of the BBC as its Charter was due to expire in December 1951. The Committee had discussed at length the central issue of whether or not the BBC's monopoly should be continued. The Committee agreed that the monopoly should be continued, but there was one dissenting voice – Mr Selwyn Lloyd, who had been a member of the 1922 Executive during the Beveridge Committee's deliberations. 'While acknowledging gladly the great gifts and high principles of those in authority at Broadcasting House,' Selwyn Lloyd had written in his minority report, 'I cannot agree that it is in the public interest that all this actual and potential influence should be vested in a public or private monopoly.' Three arguments in particular had impressed Selwyn Lloyd – first, the sheer size of the organisation made it unwieldy and hindered development; then, it was wrong to have one employer alone for broadcasters; thirdly, a monopoly in this field of expression gave excessive power to those who controlled it.

Many Members of the 1922 had been even more outspoken than Selwyn Lloyd in their criticism of the BBC. Throughout the war criticism of the BBC's left-wing bias had been expressed almost once a month at the 1922 meetings.

At the meeting on 15 November, 1951, the question of the BBC Charter renewal had first been raised by Jack Profumo, one of the most fervent advocates of competition. 'Considerable discussion followed, opinion being general that the Charter should be extended for a period of from three months to a year.' In fact, the Charter was extended for six months.

The meeting which certainly provoked the liveliest discussion and which clearly altered the course of the whole controversy, was held on 28 February, 1952. The discussion was opened by Ralph Assheton, who had been Chairman of the Party in 1945. He reminded the Committee that nearly a hundred members had recently attended another Committee to discuss the report of a small group under Jack Profumo which had recommended that the BBC monopoly should be ended. Out of the audience of one hundred, only two Members had disagreed with this recommendation.

After Sir Waldron Smithers had complained that the BBC was riddled with Communism, Reggie Maudling argued that the onus of proof was on those who wanted the BBC's monopoly continued. Richard Fort maintained that Conservative policy must favour breaking monopolies, freedom of information and freedom to choose their own entertainment. Those in favour of breaking the monopoly included Harold Watkinson, Jack Simon, and Sir Ian Fraser, a former Governor of the BBC, who emphasised the danger of a powerful leftish government using the BBC for sinister ends.

A contemporary report of the meeting records that:

> The Lord Privy Seal, Lord Salisbury, then replied to the first part of the discussion. He fully recognised the arguments in favour of ending monopoly. They fell into two categories. First that it would bring rapid technical improvement and secondly there were those who felt that monopoly was essentially bad. Lord Salisbury did not dispute these views.
>
> He said, however, that certain special features of the BBC monopoly should be taken into account if we were not to make a 'deplorable political bloomer'. First we must face the fact that there was no public demand outside the House for this change. There was no agitation in the press to end the monopoly and a wide measure of public opinion was not dissatisfied with the present set-up. The active move against monopoly was very much a House of Commons affair. He thought the Committee would be unwise to underestimate the views outside the House. He had a serious fear of vulgarization. He thought many people would prefer the BBC to remain as it is to the danger of this.
>
> We had no mandate as it was not in our programme at the General Election, and people would say that this was imposed by a House of Commons pressure group. Bitter passions would be aroused. This would be undesirable at

any time, but deplorable now, situated as we are in the midst of an economic blizzard when we shall have to take many unpopular measures. We have appealed for national unity but if now we raise this controversial issue the centre vote would be shocked and alienated and it would react most seriously on the true interests of the Party and the country.

Lord Salisbury was ready for the matter to be reconsidered as soon as the national situation made this possible, and the Government was ready to consider a period shorter than 10 years for the new Charter. In any case, he said it was improbable that much could be done for the next few years owing to material shortages. Why then risk dividing the Party at this moment when we know how very little can immediately be done. He felt the forced change would be the height of political unwisdom. He asked the Committee to realise that he had spoken in all sincerity and that they should be ready to consider objectively the views he had put before them.

There was some support for Lord Salisbury's view. Charles Doughty thought that 'our supporters were entirely against commercial broadcasting and that our present political difficulties were quite sufficient without taking on more'; but a large majority of the Committee was vehemently in favour of Jack Profumo's argument that 'a monopoly of the mind was the worst monopoly of all' and must be broken now.

At the end, Lord Woolton, the Chairman of the Party, summed up in his most avuncular 'Uncle Fred' manner:

He realised that there was a very wide difference of opinion. He himself had tried to find out true opinion in the country from correspondence and other means and from Central Office without success.

There were, he considered, two issues; those of breaking the monopoly and sponsoring. There was no monopoly except by consent, for the Postmaster General is empowered to license other Broadcasting companies. If this were to be emphasised in the new Charter would the Committee consider that it would help to meet the situation? Above all things, Lord Woolton wanted to keep the Party together. We could not afford divergences and must find a means of getting together. He referred to the difficulty of controlling sponsored programmes and the advantage they might give to the Co-ops etc. and the fact that radio advertising might drive out the small shopkeeper. How also were we to keep the Communists off the radio?

At the end of his remarks, Lord Woolton invited the 1922 Committee to convene a small group to discuss the whole issue again with Lord Salisbury and himself. At its next meeting, on 6 March, 1952, the Executive chose a group that was heavily anti-monopoly – Jack Profumo, Reggie Maudling, Niall Macpherson, Ian Orr-Ewing and John Rodgers.

The opposition to breaking the monopoly was strong. The bishops were against it, Lord Hailsham was against it. *The Times* was against it and, of course, the BBC itself was against it.

But when the Government's White Paper on broadcasting was published in May 1952, it contained one paragraph that showed that the views of the 1922 Committee had prevailed.

The present Government have come to the conclusion that in the expanding field of television, provision should be made to permit some elements of competition when the calls on capital resources at present needed for purposes of greater national importance make this feasible.

On 11 June, 1952, there was a strong debate on the Government's proposals and a furious attack launched by the Labour Party; but on 19 June, Winston Churchill nailed his own colours to the 1922 Committee's mast; '... the longer I have studied this matter and watched the developments over the last few months, the more I am convinced that the present monopoly should not continue.'

From time to time in the next eighteen months complaints were made in the 1922 Committee about delays in implementing a broadcasting policy which plainly had been decisively influenced by the meeting of 28 February, 1952.

On 4 March, 1954, the Government introduced its Bill to set up the Independent Television Authority.

On this issue, the 1922 Committee clearly had a substantial impact on the Government's thinking; but how could this influence be increased? In July 1952, the Committee discussed the question of letting Junior Ministers and Whips attend regular meetings. Junior Ministers, it was argued, should be excluded, but the Whips were invited en bloc. As Derek Walker-Smith made plain in a letter to the Chief Whip, Patrick Buchan-Hepburn, 'I ought, perhaps, to add that the invitation to be present does not confer any voting rights. Normally, as you know, votes are not taken in the 1922 Committee (the last formal vote had taken place in 1942, when the new rules had been adopted), but there is an annual vote for the election of the officers and the members of the Executive.'

On 23 April, 1953, the Committee was treated to a mild replay of the wartime fuel rationing controversy. In 1942, many Members had been instinctively apprehensive about the long-term implications of any plans produced by Socialist Ministers at the Board of Trade or the Department of Mines.

In 1952 and 1953, there were continuing doubts, in many Members' minds, about the efforts made by Conservative Ministers to deal with the problems of the nationalised industries. True Conservatives, it was argued, would devote their main energies to the problems of denationalisation rather than the problem of making the nationalised industries work. The man who bore the brunt of these criticisms was Geoffrey Lloyd, the Minister of Fuel and Power. In 1952 and 1953, the specialist back-bench Fuel and Power Committee had often been addressed by Geoffrey Lloyd and the fuel overlord, Lord Leathers, but the criticism, led by Sir Victor Raikes and Col. Claude ('Juby') Lancaster continued. The critics demanded a root-and-branch inquiry into the working of the National Coal Board, and on 23 April Geoffrey Lloyd met the critics head on in the 1922 Committee.

The confrontation was widely hailed as a smashing victory for Geoffrey Lloyd; and the demand for an inquiry died away. An official press statement at the end of the meeting noted that – 'No special action will be taken as a result of the meeting.'

It could, of course, be argued that the meeting itself had been a 'special action' and that the main 1922 Committee had been thrust into the role of a supreme court hearing the case brought by the officers of a specialist sub-group against a senior Minister in their field. It was unusual for the Committee to act in this role, but then Ministers were not often at loggerheads with the officers of their specialist committee.

After this meeting with Geoffrey Lloyd, the 1922 Committee's interest in coal and the nationalised industries dropped away. One of its major continuing interests was service pensions, and on 26 November, 1953 (just two weeks after Enoch Powell had been elected to the Executive) both the Chancellor of the Exchequer, Rab Butler, and Anthony Eden came to the Committee to head off a plea that the cuts imposed in 1935 on retired officers pensions should be restored. The Government's line was not popular: 'The Chancellor recognized the hardship' suffered by the retired officers, 'but said it was impossible to separate their claim from the claims of others. A total sum of £30m. or £40m. would be involved if we departed from the present pattern on pensions.' The discussion was not friendly, and Anthony Eden had to 'assure the Committee that the Cabinet had considered the issues at great length and the decision was a unanimous one'.

The Committee could not force the Government to increase the pensions of the retired officers, but the Executive did manage to convince the Prime Minister that his proposal for making Judges' salaries free of tax would not be acceptable. The Government would also have to listen to the Committee on the question of Members' salaries.

This became an issue again in March 1954, with the publication of the report of an authoritative committee which had been set up in July 1953, to consider the question of Members' pensions and 'the nature and extent of the expenditure incurred by Members of this House in the performance of their duties ...' The executive was invited to see the Prime Minister on this issue.

As Sir Harry Legge-Bourke recalls:

The Executive of the 1922 was by no means entirely convinced that this was an appropriate subject, but it was known that Sir Winston had wished to consider it. However, when the meeting began it soon became clear that this was not the day on which he wished to do so. After very few minutes had elapsed the Executive was regaled instead with a graphic account of the Battle of Omdurman! The

Fuzzy-Wuzzies were soon whirling in our imaginations. Lances and swords were being discarded in favour of the pistol; dust was everywhere; the din was appalling; but – almost as though by the exertions of our raconteur alone – the Battle was won. What had, perhaps, been the purpose of this vivid eye-witness account was not disclosed until later in the year, when the *Readers Digest* published a revised condensation of *My Early Life* by Winston S. Churchill. Could it have been that the text was being tried out on us to see how it would be received? Anyway, the subject of Members' salaries had to be deferred to a later day!

In fact, the discussion filled many days.

Payment to Members had begun in 1911 at a rate of £400. As David Lloyd George had said in proposing that figure – 'When we offer £400 a year as payment of Members of Parliament, it is not a recognition of the magnitude of the service ... It is just an allowance, and I think the minimum allowance to enable men to come here, men who would render incalculable service to the state and whom it is an incalculable loss to the state not to have here, but who cannot be here because their means do not allow it.'

In 1920, a Select Committee had recommended that free first class rail travel should be provided for all Members between London and their constituencies. This was soon adopted, but a recommendation that there should be free postage for Members' letters was not implemented for almost 50 years.

In June 1937, the £400 basic rate was increased to £600 and in March 1946 – following the report of yet another Select Committee – Members' pay was increased to £1,000. Junior Ministers were allowed to draw £500 of their parliamentary salary on top of their ministerial salary (before this they had lost all their parliamentary pay on taking office, a provision that still applied to senior Ministers earning £5,000 a year or more).

As soon as the report was published in February 1954, with a recommendation that Members' salaries should go up from £1,000 to £1,500, the 1922 Committee met to consider its recommendations and this discussion was carried on at a second long meeting in March.

There were two strands to the discussion. First, there was
the laudable feeling that it would be quite wrong for Members
to vote themselves what would look like an enormous rise to
most of the public when there was a threat of inflation.

On the other hand, the Maxwell-Fyfe Report adopted by the
Party some five years before had stressed that wealth should
not be an important factor when it came to selecting a candidate.
If the party was seeking able candidates without private means,
then it was surely ridiculous to expect them to live on £1,000
a year after they were elected. It could be argued that rejecting
the suggested increase would be a gesture by the rich at the
expense of the poor. Even so, the sight of grown men arguing
against an increase in their own incomes was a rare event even
in 1954.

Early in April, the Prime Minister, with Sir Anthony Eden and
Mr Butler, came to the Committee to learn at first-hand the
feeling of Members. Mr Butler opened by saying the Government proposed to make a statement in the House which would
explain that while they did not accept the salary recommendations, they were prepared to consider other means of relieving
some of the hardships of Members on both sides of the House;
for example by a system of subsistence allowances. Sir Winston
intervened at the end of the discussion. 'The Prime Minister,'
the record states, 'spoke of the desire of the Cabinet to ensure
a longer period of stable Conservative administration. He discussed the need to handle these proposals with due regard to
the tactical considerations. The condition of Parliament must
be the main consideration to be borne in mind. The Government would feel its way forward with no interest but to produce
a solution in the best interests of the country.'

This process began with the Prime Minister's announcement in the House a few days later suggesting there were
alternative methods of overcoming Members' hardship rather
than by a straight salary increase. This was badly received by
the Opposition, who pressed for a debate. The date set was
24 May, and Sir Winston decided to come again to the Committee in the interim to discuss the likely course of the debate.
With him were Mr Butler and Captain Crookshank, the Leader
of the House. Mr Butler opened with a reaffirmation of the
Government's rejection of the recommended salary increase; he

therefore advised support for a Government amendment which, in effect, would enable Members to recoup their legitimate expenses. Sir Winston, in his concluding remarks, reverted to the importance of removing undue financial pressure on Members, and stressed the advantage of a free vote.

In the event, the free vote rejected the Government's alternative by a majority of 71, and carried a resolution to increase the salary to £1,500 as recommended by the Select Committee. The confused state of opinion on the Tory side was evident when the 1922 Committee met on 27 May, the discussion ending with the Chairman's decision to ask the Prime Minister to receive the Executive at an early date. The talks took place almost at once, so that Mr Walker-Smith was able to report what had passed to the main Committee on 1 June. No less than 40 Members took part in the subsequent discussion. The matter remained officially in suspense until the Prime Minister's announcement on 24 June, 1954, that the Government was not prepared to move from its position on a salary increase 'in present circumstances', but maintained the offer to work out a system of expense allowances. The Opposition's reaction to the Government's decision was to refuse 'pairs' to Members absent from the House on official public engagements. These sanctions remained after a compromise form of allowances was announced in July.

The question of Members' pay took more of the Committee's time than any other issue in 1954 and Sir Winston Churchill's visit to discuss this subject on 20 May, 1954, proved to be his last as Prime Minister.

Even Sir Winston could not go on for ever. He resigned at the beginning of April 1955. On the evening of 5 April, the Executive met to hear Sir Patrick Spens relate the events in 1940 as he had been Chairman of the 1922 Committee when the last change of leadership took place. A discussion followed on the procedure for the election of the Leader, and it was agreed to call together the main Committee next day formally and speedily to express their thanks to the retiring Prime Minister, and to offer congratulations and assurances of support to Sir Anthony Eden. At that meeting, Sir Patrick Spens gave an appreciation of Sir Winston's services as Leader of the Party in the House of Commons. Walter Elliot then proposed that a

message of loyalty and support be sent to Sir Anthony as Prime
Minister.

The Easter break saw the newspaper strike and the announcement of the General Election. The Budget followed when
Parliament reassembled. The new Prime Minister attended the
last 1922 Committee of the Session and commended the election
manifesto to Members. On 26 May, the election result gave
Conservatives the victory with an overall majority of 60 in the
House of Commons. It was the first time in 90 years that a
Government appealing to the country after a normal term of
office had succeeded under peace-time conditions in increasing
its majority.

A unique note was struck at the opening of the first meeting
after the electoral triumph, when Sir Wavell Wakefield congratulated Central Office on their excellent work during election.
After this rare tribute, the Prime Minister attended to express
his thanks and gratification. It was a time for broad smiles and
the slapping of backs, but the dark lining to the silver cloud
was underlined by the presence of Sir Walter Monkton, the
Minister of Labour, who spoke about the menacing strike situation. The industrial scene did give some cause for alarm, but
the six meetings that remained before the summer recess could
be devoted to lesser domestic matters. Thus, when Mr Heath
announced the business on 16 June, he also 'drew attention to
a proposal of the Library Committee to alter the colour and
type of the headings on writing paper available in the House.
Members were loud-spoken and, it seemed, unanimous in their
opposition to the proposed changes'. The Committee still
respected tradition; and when Derek Walker-Smith became
Parliamentary Secretary at the Board of Trade, the Committee
chose as its new Chairman John Morrison, the Member for
Salisbury since 1942, a former High Sheriff of Wiltshire and the
cartoonist's dream of what every Chairman of the 1922 Committee should look like. Lord Lambton, then a perceptive
member of the Committee, described him as follows:

That he should have the undivided trust of the back-
benchers is in some ways surprising for he is in no way
representative of the new Conservatism.

Indeed, his main recreations are those of a nineteenth-century sporting patrician with the hounds, his shooting records and his country tastes.

The reason he goes down so well is not only that he is completely disconnected with ambition, but that in everything practical he does he excels.

Anyone who has ever watched cricket will know that a bat in the hands of Hammond or Compton or Graveney is a very different thing from one in the hands of an ordinary person. The bat seems almost mystically to become part of their body.

This can certainly be said about Major Morrison and a shotgun. He is one of those who would inevitably excel in whatever athletic activity he concentrated upon.

This, I believe, gives him an inborn confidence which reassures members of every texture in the Conservative Party, which in its turn puts him now in a position of great power.

In the week in which John Morrison became Chairman, unopposed – Enoch Powell filled the vacant vice-chairmanship – the Prime Minister, Anthony Eden, came to the Committee to defend Rab Butler's autumn budget. As the Minutes record:

He indicated that the Cabinet was completely at one in supporting the Chancellor in the measures which he proposed. Sir Anthony also discussed possible economies in the sphere of Education and Defence, and affirmed that nothing would make him change the decisions he had announced on National Service.

In conclusion, the Prime Minister said that he felt there was rough weather ahead for the Party, but he had confidence in the future if we kept to the pattern that we had designed and held to our faith.

The 'rough weather' that the Prime Minister had in mind was expected to blow most strongly on the domestic front. In the New Year successive meetings of the Committee were addressed by Oliver Poole, the new Chairman of the Party, who outlined his plans for reorganising Central Office; the new Leader of the House, Rab Butler; and the new Chief Whip, Ted Heath. They were questioned about capital punishment, teachers' superannuation, restrictive practices policy and the economic situation. The President of the Board of Trade, Peter Thorneycroft, then came to discuss his controversial Restrictive Trade Practices Bill; and he was followed by the new Chancellor of the Exchequer, Harold Macmillan, who had to describe an economic scene which was soon going to require more unpopular deflationary measures. But the two subjects which were raised most frequently during 1956 were rating and capital punishment. Both issues produced controversy and legislation.

In the five years before the outbreak of the Second World War, almost half the time of the 1922 Committee had been spent discussing some aspect of foreign affairs or defence. In the final five years of Conservative Government following the election victory of October 1951 more than 90% of the Committee's time was devoted to domestic matters. In the first half of 1956 there was some discussion of only three external issues – the sale of the Trinidad Leaseholds Oil Company to an American firm, the constitutional discussion with Malta, and the Cyprus situation.

This domestic bias did not reflect any shortage of controversy or lack of interest, but it did reflect the enhanced status of the Foreign Affairs Committee and the Commonwealth Affairs Committee. In particular, the Conservative Government's decision to attempt to negotiate a withdrawal from the Suez Canal Zone had produced a fierce reaction within a section of the Party. But just as the pre-war argument about India had been fought out in the India Committee and not in the 1922 Committee; so the argument over the withdrawal from Suez was carried on in the Foreign Affairs Committee and the Defence Committee, and not in the main 1922 Committee. The issue had been raised obliquely on 3 December, 1953, when

> Brigadier Prior Palmer raised the matter of a press report to the effect that certain members of the Party were preparing a memorandum to send to the Prime Minister.
>
> Brigadier Prior Palmer maintained that this was by-passing the Party Committee dealing with the subject, and also by-passing the 1922 Committee.
>
> Captain Waterhouse replied that the report referred to a private meeting and emphasized the right of private

members to write to the Prime Minister or any other Minister with or without the co-operation of other members of the Party. Discussion followed.

The opponents of British withdrawal from the Canal Zone could write memoranda to their hearts' content, but these memoranda went unheeded. In June 1956, the last contingent of British troops left the Canal Zone.

On 26 July, Sir Anthony Eden made the traditional Prime Ministerial end-of-term speech to the Committee. It was the traditional review of the Session's accomplishments and problems. After leaving the Committee at 7 p.m., the Prime Minister changed for the dinner that he was giving for the King of Iraq and the Prime Minister, Nuri Al-Said, one of Britain's staunchest allies in the Middle East. In the middle of dinner a Private Secretary entered with the news that President Nasser had nationalised the Suez Canal Company.

As the negotiations and the military planning went on, Parliament reassembled in the middle of September for a brief, acrimonious debate. As one member put it, 'The Labour Party was afraid that the Government would use force. The 1922 Committee was afraid that the Government wouldn't.' Some Junior Ministers were allowed to attend the special meeting of the Committee on 13 September, when the Minutes record:

> The Prime Minister and the Foreign Secretary were welcomed by the Chairman. The Prime Minister made a short statement about the Suez Canal negotiations. He invited Members to express their opinions. Many Members addressed the Committee. The Prime Minister replied to the more important points before leaving the Foreign Secretary to reply to the remaining matters.

At the first meeting of the Committee when the House reassembled in the autumn, there was no direct reference to the crisis; but from then on, following the Anglo-French ultimatum and the sailing of the expeditionary force, the meetings of the 1922 Committee and the Foreign Affairs Committee virtually became indistinguishable.

On 8 November, after the cease fire, the Minutes read:

> The Foreign Secretary was given an ovation. He gave the

Committee an account of the situation in the Middle East
and outlined the proposals of the Government for the
immediate future. Many Members addressed questions to
the Foreign Secretary. Mr Selwyn Lloyd dealt with the
numerous points raised.

The Minutes record opaquely the progress of the discussion
within the Committee. Thus, on 15 November, 'Sir Wavell
Wakefield explained the steps he had taken to deal with critical
supporters who had written protesting against the Middle East
policy of the Government. Other Members spoke.'

On 22 November, 'The Chairman reported that the Officers
of the 1922 Committee had been to see the Prime Minister in
his bedroom at Downing Street, and that apart from exhaustion
they had found him extremely well ... Mr Butler and Mr Macmillan addressed the meeting on the situation in the Middle East
and explained the Government's views. The Lord Privy Seal
(Mr Butler) announced the Government's intentions to overhaul
the Government's publicity arrangements.

On 29 November, 'The Foreign Secretary attended the Committee. He was accompanied by the Lord Privy Seal, the Chancellor of the Exchequer and the Chief Whip. The Foreign
Secretary gave an account of his visit to the United States, and
reported on recent developments in the Middle East situation.
He answered a number of questions addressed to him by members
of the Committee.'

On Thursday, 6 December, 'Sir Thomas Moore drew attention to the repercussions that might arise if there were a
substantial number of abstentions on the vote to be taken that
evening on the Government's action at Suez. A large number
of Members spoke on this issue. Captain Waterhouse explained
why he intended to abstain.'

The meeting on 13 December was devoted to a discussion
of the Homicide Bill, but on 20 December 'The Chairman
introduced the Prime Minister who made a general statement
on the situation leading up to Britain's action in the Middle
East and the consequences. He thanked the Party for their
loyalty, and answered questions for 45 minutes. The Prime
Minister was warmly applauded by the Committee. The Chairman conveyed the thanks of the Committee to the Prime Minister

and expressed to him and Lady Eden the best wishes for Christmas.'

The Committee's applause was not strong enough to sustain the Prime Minister through his illness. When the 1922 met again after the Christmas recess, on 24 January, 1957, the Chairman 'read the Committee a telegram of good wishes sent to Sir Anthony Eden and a message of congratulations sent to the new Prime Minister'.

The matter-of-fact words of the Minute Books do not convey any picture of the tension generated within the Committee in the last two months of 1956. One Member of the Committee who had been abroad on a delegation, and who did not return until the end of November, described the atmosphere. 'It was rather like going on board a steamer at the end of a very rough crossing. There was a slight smell of sickness in the Smoking Room and almost everyone looked green.'

The Minute on 22 November that 'Mr Butler and Mr Macmillan addressed the meeting on the situation in the Middle East and explained the Government's views' recalls in the plainest terms one of the classic confrontations in the history of the 1922 Committee. As one Member recalled – 'Rab announced a change in the publicity machinery, while Harold made a bid for the leadership which we knew was coming into question. It was a real leadership speech.' As one of the Whips present recalled 'Rab was not on his best form, whereas Harold was at his most ebullient and managed to win the day, not only on the merit of what he said (as it seemed to the Committeee) but also physically in that his expansive gestures nearly caused poor Rab to fall backwards from the adjacent seat.'

In fact the 250 Members who were present at this confrontation had little direct part to play in the choice of Sir Anthony Eden's successor which was, in practice, handled by the Cabinet itself. Junior Ministers had been specially invited to the meeting, and Parliamentary Private Secretaries reported the evening's events to their Ministers. Indeed this confrontation soon became part of the 1922 Committee folklore, but the Cabinet Ministers who were soon to be asked the question 'Is it Rab or Harold?' were not at the meeting. It is doubtful whether any of the votes in the Cabinet were influenced by that confrontation.

There were some who thought that the succession would prove to be brief. As one senior officer of the 1922 Committee at the time remarked, 'I doubted whether the Government could survive for three weeks.'

The fact that the Government survived so easily when the prospects seemed so daunting can be laid in some small part to Mr Macmillan's 1922 strategy. If he was to impress his personality on the country the easiest route lay in first impressing the House, and if he was to impress the House, he must first impress his own followers in the House. It would be an exaggeration to say that the Prime Minister was always popping in to talk to the 1922 Committee during the first year, but that was the impression he gave. He appeared almost as often as his predecessor, Sir Anthony Eden, who attended no less than six of the thirty-nine meetings of the 1922 Committee held while he was Prime Minister, but the election and the Suez crisis accounted for more than half of these.

In the period of party reconstruction that followed on Mr Macmillan's arrival at 10 Downing Street divisive issues tended to receive a low priority – after protests in the Committee, the Shops Bill was dropped – and meetings of the 1922 Committee became, for a period, non-controversial and positively dull. Even the old bones of contention hardly seemed worth chewing over. When the decision to implement the recommendations of the 1954 Select Committee on Members' pay was announced in the middle of the summer of 1957, there was hardly a murmur of dissent.

When the new Session began in October there was an appeal by Henry Price for volunteers to play ping pong in Paris against a team of French Deputies, and John Boyd-Carpenter, the Minister of Pensions, was able to stress to the Committee that the increase in the pensions that he had just announced was the largest single increase which had ever been introduced. At the next meeting, Ernest Marples, the Postmaster General, was congratulated on the way he had announced the forthcoming reduction in telephone charges. Things seemed undoubtedly to be looking up. In April 1958, the Government even seemed to win an industrial confrontation when the London busmen returned to work after a long and unpopular strike.

At the first meeting of the Committee at the beginning of

the 1958-59 Session, Mr Dudley Williams urged his colleagues not to attend the Liberal Party Annual Ball, and the Committee continued in a minor key. Colonel Richard Glyn hoped that the Meat (Staining and Sterilisation) Regulations would not be implemented and Robin Turton feared that the new agreement with Denmark would adversely effect British pig farmers, but the real controversy was rare. The Committee and the country seemed content.

On 23 July, 1959, Alan Lennox-Boyd addressed a crowded meeting on the report into the killing by some Kenya prison warders of a number of Mau Mau suspects at Hola prison camp. But this was a small cloud. Inside and outside the 1922 Committee 'Supermac' seemed to reign supreme, and at the General Election on Thursday, 8 October, the Conservative Party increased its majority to 100. If there were precedents for a Government increasing its majority at two consecutive General Elections, the experts could not think of them.

8

The Bona Vista
(1959-64)

WHEN THE COMMITTEE MET for the first time after this third consecutive victory 'The Prime Minister, who was given a very warm welcome, spoke for 15 minutes on the result of the General Election'. As one Member recalls 'It was a perfectly relaxed speech and then, at the very end, he seemed to miss his cue to sit down and he got that glassy look that some garden party openers get when they don't know how to finish, and they search desperately for a peroration.'

But at this stage the Committee would not have minded if the Prime Minister had forgotten all his perorations. The old problems and the old enemies seemed, for the moment, to have been defeated while the new problems and new enemies had not yet arisen. This was the moment when some experts were predicting that the Conservative Party would have to provide its own opposition as the Labour Party in defeat would become an incompetent rabble.

In fact, Mr Macmillan took care not to neglect the Committee. On 18 February, 1960, it is recorded that the Prime Minister 'received an ovation' after his return from his African tour, a trip which reinforced his intention of disentangling Great Britain as quickly as possible from her African possessions. Within a month, on 11 March, he was back, with Ernest Marples, to talk about the problems of British Railways. On 28 April, he had a more congenial task of discussing with the Committee some of his hopes for the forthcoming Summit Conference and the Commonwealth Conference. In the event the Summit Conference in Paris broke up in some disorder, and Mr Macmillan's best laid plans for the orderly conduct of foreign policy were confounded.

It was not only at the summit that difficulties arose, for the

1960-1 Session was to see the emergence of three issues which were, intermittently, to dominate much of British politics for the next 12 years – immigration, the Common Market, and incomes policy.

At the first Committee meeting of the Session 'Sir John Vaughan Morgan raised the question of the inordinate length of opposition speeches in the House'. The Opposition now had plenty to talk about.

In retrospect, it may seem curious that the first serious discussion of immigration by the Committee was not held until 8 December, 1960, when the subject was raised by Cyril Osborne. On 22 June, 1961, the Lord Privy Seal, Mr Heath, gave the first of his reports on the Common Market situation. In the following week there was a discussion on rising prices that foreshadowed the introduction into the English language of words like 'pay pause' and 'incomes policy'.

All these issues were likely to put a strain on Party unity and the Commonwealth Immigration Bill soon produced massive argument. On 16 November, 1961, Iain Macleod came to the Committee for a discussion which centred on the Irish question. There could be no doubt that the overwhelming majority of the Committee wanted immigration from the Irish Republic to be controlled in the Bill, and Iain Macleod, who had not endeared himself to the right wing of the Party during his term as Colonial Secretary, was solidly on the defensive. He acknowledged the force of the argument that Irish immigration should be covered. He doubted, however, whether a practical method of control could be found, since it would be impossible to police the Eire-Ulster border.

The tactical handling of the Bill was discussed at a number of meetings, but it was not the only issue that brought Iain Macleod into close contact with the Committee. On 8 March, he returned to defend the Government's decision to set up yet another all-Party Committee which would discuss the composition of the House of Lords. The issue had been brought to the boil by the energetic resistance against translation from the House of Commons to the House of Lords put up by Anthony Wedgwood Benn when he succeeded his father as Lord Stansgate. Anthony Wedgwood Benn had fought and won a by-election in his old Bristol constituency in May 1961, but the Election

Court had ruled, in July 1961, that the new Lord Stansgate was debarred from sitting in the House of Commons.

A clear majority of the hundred Members present at the Committee to discuss Lords reform seemed to be opposed to any action. The majority view was put succinctly by Charles Doughty. Why should we bother? We would only look foolish in the country, as it would seem that we had been forced into it by Wedgwood Benn. Despite Iain Macleod's arguments, virtually his only ally in support of the Government's proposals was Sir Godfrey Nicholson, who thought the all-Party Committee an excellent idea because it would not report for many years, and nothing need be done about it in the end.

Meanwhile, the Committee had been disturbed by a number of developments in Africa. In November 1961, the Queen had been due to visit Ghana. The President of Ghana, Kwame Nkrumah, had for some time become increasingly unpopular with a substantial section of the Ghanaian population, and there were fears that the Queen's safety would be put in jeopardy. On 8 November, 1961, the Chief Whip warned Mr Macmillan that there was a growing feeling in the Conservative Party against the Queen's visit. On the information available, Mr Macmillan felt that he must advise that the visit should go ahead, but for a time it seemed that the House of Commons would vote to reject his advice – a situation which would have provoked a complex constitutional crisis. In fact the Queen's visit passed off uneventfully and successfully. There was no adverse vote and as Mr Macmillan noted in his *Memoirs*:

> Fortunately, the instigators of this revolt in the Conservative ranks were very *good* men – worthy men, and only caring about the Queen's safety. It was led by John Morrison, Spencer Summers, and others of the same kind. John Morrison is, of course, *very* influential as Chairman of 1922. None of these are of the self-advertising or embittered type ... So *nothing at all* got into the Press up to the end ...*

The next Party revolt on Africa contained more heat and bitterness. At the end of November 1961, relations between the United Nations force in the Congo and the secessionist state

* Harold Macmillan, *Pointing The Way*, pp. 469-70 (Macmillan 1972).

of Katanga had deteriorated sharply, and fighting broke out. On 7 December, 1961, the British Cabinet decided to supply the United Nations forces with twenty-four 1,000 lb. bombs. Mr Tshombe, the head of the Katangan Government, had a number of supporters in the Conservative Party, and the Cabinet decision provoked a short, sharp, political crisis. As Mr Macmillan wrote to the Queen on 13 December:

> Your Majesty will have seen the trouble we got into over the Congo. I will be quite frank, and say that I think we were put into an impossible position by the United Nations Secretariat last week. We were given the impression that their troops were in a rather desperate condition and unless these bombs could be made available we would become responsible for their being in a perilous, and perhaps a fatal situation. Very reluctantly, therefore, all the more reluctantly because we knew these were not the instruments which any skilful Air Force would use, but subject to the conditions which we obtained in writing, we agreed to send them. The 1,000 lb bomb however became the detonator of a kiloton row in the House of Commons.*

The 1922 Executive was summoned to see Mr Macmillan and after the debate on Thursday the internal party controversy subsided, but the Government had been shaken.

While many members of the 1922 Committee were momentarily occupied with African affairs, the electorate was increasingly aware of domestic difficulties. On 14 March, 1962, the Party suffered a stunning defeat at the Orpington by-election. On 22 March, Iain Macleod was back yet again to reply to a post mortem on the loss of Orpington and the near loss of a safe seat in Blackpool. The discussion was opened by Roger Gresham Cooke, whose constituency of Twickenham was not wholly unlike Orpington. A record of the meeting noted that:

> Roger Gresham Cooke said ... It was true that the Government was very unpopular and that our supporters were voting Liberal. They did so for illogical reasons. They complained that we were not tough enough with the Trade Unions and were against the pay pause. They complained

* Harold Macmillan, *Pointing The Way*, p. 450 (Macmillan 1972).

about the treatment of teachers' pay, and yet were cross when the rates went up. They thought that we were not taking a lead.

Albert Cooper had discovered in Orpington that paid-up Tory members were voting Liberal, but he did not think that the Liberals represented a danger at a General Election. For the last year Ministers had not disturbed themselves at weekends to explain policy.

Dame Irene Ward complained that any new idea now seems to get sat on, for example, the idea of a Committee to discuss a new approach to rating. The country was apprehensive over our alleged failure to deal with the Unions. Conservative supporters were not represented on NEDC; they did not like their future being decided by it. The Chancellor should have included professional bodies, and maybe a representative of consumers. Professional people cannot understand the pay pause. They cannot increase their productivity.

Geoffrey Hirst regarded Orpington as worse than our recent election setbacks at Tonbridge, and Torrington. Those had been a revolt of the extreme right. This time there was a general sense of discontent in the middle classes. The Government was thought to have lost its sense of mission. The policies were not wrong, but there was a lack of courage, conviction and explanation in carrying them out.

Douglas Glover considered Orpington was the revolt of the unorganised against the organised. Our attitude towards the Trade Unions had not won us support. The Party must have a tighter grip on Ministerial activities from now on. From the time the pay pause was announced in July, until the House came back in the autumn, how many members of the Government had spoken in favour of it?

Nigel Fisher pointed out that people voted Liberal for odd reasons, even those against the Common Market and against any immigration. It could not be said that this was a vote for the Liberals; it was a vote against us. Schedule 'A' Tax, high mortgage interest rates, the cost of season tickets on suburban trains, all worry the young married. There were many civil servants in Orpington who had been affected by the pay pause, and who were angry at the failure of the Government to keep within its expenditure targets. As a Government, we had not helped the middle classes.

Charles Doughty said the people in Orpington were living close to the financial limit. They had houses to buy, mortgages, season tickets and fuel, all of which had gone up without explanation. Sometimes they could not even get mortgages now. We had been elected on a 'property owning democracy' campaign. Now these people thought we were letting them down. They thought that the Government dared not enforce the pay pause against the Unions.

Philip Goodhart was much impressed with the absence of bitterness as compared with the 1957/58 slump, but there was a great boredom with us. Particularly amongst those under 45, it was no longer avant-garde to vote Tory. We needed a theme, but he did not know how we could decide on this until we knew how the Common Market would go.

Humphry Berkeley asked whether Central Office had been astonished by the result at Orpington? He had seen the canvass returns, and he considered our techniques were now wrong. Or had the electors been deliberately deceitful? We did have more cars than the Liberals, but the only trouble was that we ferried Liberals to the Poll.

Mr Macleod, replying, agreed that the feeling now was less bitter than in 1957, but the situation was more serious. We would not be so fortunate this time. After all, we had been helped by a number of advantageous factors at that time, especially the London bus strike.

Torrington had been the last of a bad series. This time things would get worse before they got better, and some of the by-elections to come would be very bad.

People voted Liberal for wholly illogical reasons. They were the faceless men of politics. It had been traditional to ignore the Liberals. He thought this was now wrong and we must start attacking the Liberals and try to pin them down on policy.

The pay pause outweighed all other subjects by nine to one in his post-Orpington postbag, but policies fundamentally unpopular could not be presented popularly. The policy was wholly right, but very unpopular, and unfor-

tunately the Orpington type of constituency was worst hit
by it. There was a feeling that the very rich and the Unions
could opt out and the middle classes had been sacrificed.
Frankly, they had been.

The policies were now beginning to show success. There
was a genuine belief abroad that we were solving our
economic problems. The trade prospects were brighter than
for a very long time, and the cut in the Bank Rate to-day
was a sign of this.

It was certainly true that it was difficult to sell our
policies as long as there was a lack of finality about the
Common Market decision.

He continued to have a fierce faith in the mission of
the Tory Party, and he believed our policies were right,
and in due course would be seen to be right.

Perhaps the Common Market negotiations would be concluded
in time to give the Party a new impetus.

In the following week, the Lord Privy Seal, Edward Heath,
gave a progress report on the negotiations with the European
Economic Community. It was recorded in the Minutes that
'Mr Heath delivered a very long and complicated speech which
had a very favourable reception'.

There was immense confidence within the Community
itself [Mr Heath reported]. They even took the view that if
British problems had not been solved exactly right (during
the negotiations) they could easily be adapted once Britain
was in. They wondered why the British Government could
not share this flexible attitude.

Much of the discussion in the Committee centred on
agriculture, and Mr Heath reported that 'we had told the Community that we would not join in their agricultural discussion ...
unless and until we became Members. We had to remove suspicions that we wanted to impede the progress of the Community;
at the same time the Community was worried that if we finally
decided not to come in they might be left with a structure that
really did not suit them.'

The Committee was now increasingly preoccupied with Party

images and there was much discussion of the failure of communication between the Front Bench and the back-benches. On 3 May, 1962, Martin Redmayne, the Chief Whip, opened a discussion on liaison within the Party. As a Chief Whip, he knew that the best way to improve communications is to promote a number of back-benchers to the front benches at regular intervals – but no-one then contemplated a Government reconstruction quite as large as the one made necessary by the 'night of the long knives' on 13 July, 1962, when Selwyn Lloyd and five other Cabinet Ministers were removed from their posts.

On 19 July, the Prime Minister saw the Executive for their regular end-of-term meeting, and then came to the main Committee. The first topic of conversation with the Executive was the Common Market. Here the Prime Minister was confident. The Lord Privy Seal had been conducting the negotiations very skilfully. Mr Macmillan hoped by the end of July or early in August to have a broad picture of the terms. They would have to see what came out of Brussels in August. The Commonwealth Prime Ministers Conference would begin on 10 September. After that they would decide.

The discussion on incomes policy and the dismissal of the Chancellor was sharper. At times the 1922 Executive may be open to the charge of making an excessively deferential approach in its contacts with the Prime Minister of the day, but there was little sign of undue deference at that particular meeting.

The Chancellor goes and we have a new piano, but why are we playing the same tune? If this is a continuation of the Selwyn Lloyd policy, why get rid of Selwyn Lloyd? Wouldn't it have been better if the Ministers had sent proper letters of resignation and not been pushed aside? The country had been given the impression that we were panicking. Couldn't Selwyn Lloyd have been made Home Secretary?

The Prime Minister's replies were defensive. 'I have the greatest admiration for the work Selwyn did, but I felt we needed a new team of younger men. I will carry on for the time being. History will show whether it has been right or wrong. It was a very painful decision to make ... I am Leader of the

Party and I decided to do it. I was not going to let it drift.
I did what I thought was right.'

There were elements of drama and tragedy in the dismissal
of almost half of the Cabinet, but the Session ended on a note
of pure farce. The annual lunch for the Prime Minister at the
Savoy was held at the very end of the Session in 1962. Because
of the recent ministerial changes, there was unusual interest in
what the Prime Minister would say and an unusual preoccupation with security. There is a stage at the side of the dining-
room at the Savoy. The curtains were drawn across the stage,
but shortly before the Prime Minister began to speak, Sir
Charles Taylor peered behind the curtain. There, with pencil
poised, sat a press officer of the Savoy with a companion. 'The
ladies behind the curtain' created a momentary sensation, but
there were few other excuses for laughter. The economic situation seemed easier, but unexpected misfortunes continued to
press upon the Government.

At the 1922 Committee's meeting on 8 November, 1962,
'Dame Irene Ward opened a discussion on the Vassall case
and Mr Galbraith's resignation'. Vassall, a clerk in the Admiralty,
had been arrested as a spy. He had worked as a clerk for Tam
Galbraith, a junior Minister at the Admiralty, and wild allegations were made about a relationship between the Minister and
the clerk. Tam Galbraith had resigned pending the enquiry,
and it was widely believed that the Government's relations with
important sections of the press had been soured by the whole
exercise.

The Vassall case and its aftermath was a temporary sensation,
and Tam Galbraith was wholly vindicated. A more damaging
blow to the Government's momentum was noted, on 31 January,
1963, when 'Mr Edward Heath spoke to the Committee about
the breakdown of the Common Market negotiations in Brussels
and answered questions'. Even the climate seemed to have turned
against the Government, and an exceptionally severe winter
helped to push the unemployment figures momentarily above the
million mark.

On 17 June, 1963, 'Lord Poole opened a discussion on the
Profumo case and the Chief Whip answered questions'. It had
been alleged that Jack Profumo, the Secretary of State for War,
had been associating with Miss Christine Keeler, a night club

hostess. Miss Keeler's clients were also said to include a Soviet Naval Attaché. Jack Profumo had first denied and then admitted the affaire. There was widespread criticism of the Government's handling of the issue.

Inevitably, there was talk of a change of leadership, and on 20 June, 1963, the *Daily Telegraph* carried a report of a poll conducted by its political correspondent, Harry Boyne:

A sample opinion poll, taken privately among 50 MPs, leaves no doubt that they want to see Mr Maudling as Prime Minister.

The MPs, representing a fair cross-section of the party's strength, were asked to name their first choice for Mr Macmillan's successor. On the assumption that all Conservative MPs would vote as the sample did, the resultant figures are:

'Mr Maudling – 147; Viscount Hailsham – 56; Mr Heath – 42; Mr Butler – 28; Mr Powell – 21; Earl of Home and Mr Macleod – 7 each. No firm choice – 35 ...'

In the inner circle of the '1922' Committee, it is reliably estimated that between 60 and 70 per cent of Conservative MPs are ready to support Mr Maudling.

By the time that Mr Macmillan was ready to make his end-of-session speech to the 1922 Committee on 25 July, much of the fever had abated. The meeting coincided with the initialling of the test ban treaty in Moscow, but inevitably interest centred on more domestic issues such as the Profumo débâcle.

Notes for this meeting had been prepared with great care.

With hindsight, it is easy to think, or for the critics to say, that it should have been handled differently. Whether that is true or not, or whether, in fact, it is not a greater virtue to believe the word of a colleague, is now irrelevant. What matters is that the disclosure of the truth was a great shock to the Party and that its timing, coming as it did during the Whitsun recess, and being debated immediately thereafter, was just as difficult as it could be. This shock to the system has put a great strain on us all.

I am well aware that, under the stress of these conditions,

many of you have said that it is time for a change in the leadership, and in respect of that let me say, straightly, that any decision which I may reach will be based wholly on my assessment of what is right and good for the Party and for the nation.

What we have got to do is to win the next election. In order to win the next election, we must be poised as a united party under the strongest leadership available to us. Our policies must be forward-looking, well presented, highly political in content and, if possible, strongly contrasted to those of the Socialists. Further, the public appreciation of them must not be distracted by irrelevancies of rumour and scandal.

I can tell you that when the pressures against me were at their highest, I was sorely tempted to throw up the sponge. Had I done so, I would have been guilty of a crime against the Conservative Party and against my colleagues. My first responsibility, whatever may follow, is to see that this bogey of rumour and scandal, which has pursued us throughout the whole of this year, and particularly during the last few months, is finally destroyed. It would be unthinkable that I should allow any successor to be saddled with this additional burden.

If one is to consider change, one must consider also the timing of it. It is a nice thought that one can change a Prime Minister, reform a Government, recast policies and press on through a full parliamentary year to assured electoral success. I have been in this game a long time, and believe me it does not work out that way. Admittedly, you have got to build up the image of your new man. I am not sure that my image, in my turn, in the years leading up to 1959 was not *too* well presented. 'SuperMac' is a splendid illusion, but a difficult position to maintain through seven long years. You might well think, therefore, that if the timing is to be right, it ought to be based first on a decision as to when an election should be held, and then, by working back from that, to take account of the optimum period required to build up the image of a new man. The time can be unduly exaggerated or, on the other hand, damaged by some unavoidable misfortune. This is worth consideration.

Another factor is the choice itself. The transition from one leader to another man has got to be smooth, and the Party must know its mind. I tell you, frankly, that I should be most reluctant to lay down my responsibilities until I was sure that the Party, under its new Leader, was going to be more certain, more strong, more united than it was before the change.

Various theories have been voiced as to how certainty of choice is to be achieved. I do ask you to consider carefully the constitutional effects of some of them. No one in this room can deny that it is The Queen who has the right of choice, and although it may seem an attractive proposition that she should be guided by foreknowledge of what man would be acceptable to the Party, if we were to insist too firmly on such procedure, we might well do damage, which in the years to come could lead to the destruction of the Monarchy. What is guidance to-day might be dictatorship by a political party to-morrow, and, at a time when the balance of political power was very much more extreme than it is to-day, there could be real danger that The Queen might be forced by these procedures to send for a man whose political beliefs could put the whole safety of the Nation at stake.

Nevertheless, I appreciate that where there is not an heir apparent, I must be sure that in due course one is forthcoming, and I give you my word that I shall not give up until I know that, by the various proper methods of communications which are open to us, the Party will accept a man who may be called as my successor, and accept him with goodwill and with the certain knowledge that their views have been fully assessed and fully taken into account. All this can be perfectly well achieved if, discarding the passions of these last few weeks, you will trust my intention to see that they are done. So much, then, for that. I say again, my whole concern, whether I stay or whether I go, will be to see that what is done and the method of doing it is in the best interests of the Party.

In fact the notes which Mr Macmillan took with him into the Committee were considerably shorter.

Usual Session. Important Bills. Reflation without inflation. Scotland, North East, Mersey-side. Budget; mill at Fort William; £60 million scheme for shipbuilding; modernisation of Britain; Defence.

12 years 3 Elections. Pride but brings its own problems. Internal – Parliamentary Party, external – public opinion. Mr Butler and I only survivors of Sir Winston's postwar Administration. 204/members of Conservative Administration/people in 12 years. In House of Commons, 32 first came 1951 of whom 27 remain. 51 first came 1955, of whom 49 remain.

1951 majority of 16. 1955 we had 50. Now we have 100.

1945 apparatus of a war economy. Gradual decontrol. 1957/58 economic difficulties. By 1959 resolved. Third victory extravagant expectations, 1961 halt. Europe same problems repudiating debt and devaluing. Now even the U.S.

Election partly on our record.

(1) Colonial Empire into Commonwealth Central Africa.
(2) Peace: Berlin, Summit and U.2; Test ban.
(3) Prosperity: defence of Affluence.

New enthusiasms.

Profumo. If I had resigned division in Party and damage abroad. Realised not only in own Party but in Opposition. Denning Report.

My intention? Always put Party and country first.

A full report of the meeting by the political correspondent of *The Times* noted that:

In all, Mr Macmillan spoke or answered questions for 40 minutes. There are varying descriptions of his reception. Some reports speak of a most cordial reception, of cheering and the thumping of desk tops. Others noted that about a quarter of the audience were not demonstrative, and that no-one followed the example of Sir Walter Bromley-Davenport when he rose to his feet to cheer the Prime Minister's entry. It seems possible that Conservative leaders have received greater ovations at an end-of-term occasion like this.

The comment was that Mr Macmillan had not enjoyed a Roman triumph ...

Meanwhile, some soundings had already been taken through 'the various proper methods of communications which are open to us' to ascertain who the heir apparent might be. John Morrison, who had by now served longer as Chairman of the 1922 Committee than anyone since Sir Gervais Rentoul, had already made extensive enquiries about back-bench preferences if Harold Macmillan should decide to retire. At the same time, Harry Boyne, the Political Correspondent of the *Daily Telegraph*, was conducting another wide-ranging poll of his own. The result of both the published and unpublished polls was the same. Reggie Maudling, the Chancellor of the Exchequer, seemed to have a commanding lead. The Boyne poll of 100 members showed 71 supporting Mr Maudling, against the 9 for Rab Butler, 5 for Lord Hailsham and 1 each for Ted Heath and Enoch Powell.

The Chairman's enquiries also produced one important negative result. At the end of June, John Morrison called on Rab Butler, just before the First Secretary was due to leave for Rhodesia, where he was to preside over the Conference which was to ratify the unravelling of the Central African Federation. John Morrison's message for Rab Butler was simple and direct – 'the chaps won't have you'. On his return from the Victoria Falls Conference, Rab Butler naturally asked friends on the Executive whether John Morrison's assessment was accurate. The answer was a bleak 'yes'.

John Morrison had one other call to make. On the day that the House of Lords Reform Bill reached the Statute Book, he went to see Lord Home, the Foreign Secretary. Once again the message was simple. Now that it was possible for peers to disclaim their titles and return to the House of Commons, the demands of party unity might make it desirable and even necessary that the Foreign Secretary should become Leader. Lord Home was sceptical. John Morrison was insistent, and in the end the Foreign Secretary gave a reply that left all the options open: 'I will see my doctor.'

During the summer recess, talk of resignation faded away, but as the delegates were assembling at Blackpool for the Conservative Party's Annual Conference, the Prime Minister was rushed to hospital to have an emergency operation for prostatic obstruction.

As the Parliamentary Correspondent of *The Times* described the opening of the Conference:

> In an atmosphere of bemused unreality, as though delegates had been stunned by the news of the night before, the Conservative Party Conference opened here to-day and went through the motions of its business. There was little to cheer, little to raise electioneering fervour. Beside the overriding issue of the party leadership, being hotly discussed at so many private meetings that the platform at times was almost emptied, all else seemed irrelevant and insignificant.
>
> Only one of the fancied contenders was present – Lord Hailsham. He arrived with typical panache at the moment when the rest of the platform introductions had been completed, to meet an ovation which he received with more obvious pleasure than some of his colleagues.
>
> It was the only chance the delegates had to show their feelings on the matter, and they took it.

It was decided, on the evening of Wednesday, 9 October, that Rab Butler, the Deputy Prime Minister, would address the mass rally on the Saturday, after the Conference closed. Meanwhile, David Wood, *The Times* Political Correspondent, assessed the chances of the other main candidates:

> Mr Maudling, when Parliament dispersed at the beginning of August, could have commanded a majority among backbenchers in the Commons. Lord Hailsham, as his reception showed to-day, on his first appearance before the conference, continues to be the darling of the constituency associations. A fourth, hypothetical candidate, Lord Home, would probably be the choice in perfection of the party's organisation men, simply because he combines with traditional Conservative qualities the advantage that a majority throughout the party could compromise on him. Senior Ministers have made it quite clear that Lord Home has no wish to enter the contest. His role is expected to be that of king maker.

While the newspapers were speculating, principally on the chances of Rab Butler and Lord Hailsham, John Morrison had a quiet talk with the Chancellor of the Exchequer, Reggie Maudling, and told him that the party leadership was in his grasp.

Thursday was certainly Lord Hailsham's day. His speech at the Conservative Political Centre provoked a thunderous response and his announcement that he was prepared to renounce his title in order to seek the leadership brought a near-hysterical response. Applause alone would not choose the next leader, but Lord Hailsham's reception certainly helped to make the Party unduly applause-conscious. As one commentator put it, 'Some sort of standing ovation at a conference had become a minimum qualification for entry in the leadership stakes.'

Reggie Maudling's opportunity came on Friday, when he replied to the economic debate. He began with a declaration that he did not share the views of those who decried the value of material prosperity. There was no grandeur in poverty, and the purpose of economic advance must be to liberate man from the bonds of poverty, as they had largely done in Britain, and then to free them from the shackles of drudgery and frustration ... But what was the purpose of this effort?

The nation must not jog along, but be inspired with the determination to achieve great things.

Where did this inspiration lie? Not in natural prosperity alone, important as that was. Whatever his income, a man was only half alive if he did not take a pride in his job and if he did not have a sense of service to others. And this was the theme that had grown throughout the conference – pride and service.

The Times noted that

If nobody is yet quite sure how the Conservative Party is going to select its new leader, at least it seems fairly certain that it will not be done by one of those machines which measure the volume of applause. Mr Maudling, for one, had good reason to feel relieved about this today. Were it so, then on this morning's showing, the next Prime Minister would be the fourteenth Earl of Home, with the present Chancellor well down among the also-rans.

Mr Maudling, it must be recorded, had only himself to blame. As the first serious contender for the throne to address the conference since Mr Macmillan's announcement, he was confidently expected to close the economic debate with a rousing speech. It did not happen.

With the economic tide flowing the Government's way at last, and with a personal incentive as great as any man could ask for, this was surely a moment for sounding the brass. Mr Maudling had left the mute stuck in his trumpet.

The reactions which followed his speech were amusing, instructive, or depressing, depending on one's personal point of view. The clapping started slowly, grew to a moderate volume, and there it stuck. In an effort to get the bandwagon moving, a few of Mr Maudling's supporters on the platform, and a sparse scattering in the body of the hall, jumped to their feet and cheered. But the bulk of the conference would not be budged. They stuck to their seats and damned the Chancellor with faint praise. One by one, the Maudlingites faltered and sat down.

By contrast, the standing ovation which had been given to Lord Home a short while before was made to look the more remarkable. His speech on foreign affairs had been able and witty, its delivery crisp and assured. In content it contained not a whit more news than that of Mr Maudling, yet it qualified Lord Home for the sort of thunderous reception which Mr Macleod earned yesterday.

In the context of the leadership battle, did this mean anything or nothing? Lord Hailsham, who for some reason of his own spent the morning down among the delegates (but in comfortable view of the cameras), would probably like to know.

Lord Home remains magnificently non-committal on the possibility of his candidature. Today, he offered a prize to any reporter who could find a single clue in his speech, and it will certainly go unclaimed.

Before the mass really to be addressed by Rab Butler on Saturday, the 1922 Committee Executive met at the Bona Vista hotel, a modest establishment into which Sir Richard Nugent had been booked by his agent. The 20-room Bona Vista, standing on the front one mile north of the main conference hotel, was not luxurious, but it was inconspicuous. The unexpected arrival of a coach party pushed the Executive from the lounge into the bar, where they were joined by Martin Redmayne, the Chief Whip in the House of Commons, and Lord St Aldwyn, the Chief Whip in the House of Lords. The absentees from the meeting included Charles Mott-Radclyffe, one of the Vice-Chairmen, Arthur Vere-Harvey, who was in a room almost next door to Harold Macmillan at the King Edward VII Hospital, and one of the Secretaries, Philip Goodhart, who was on the UN delegation in New York. It seems that, at the outset, two of those present still supported Maudling and two supported Lord Hailsham. The rest leaned heavily towards Lord Home. Soon there was virtual unanimity that Lord Home was the one candidate likely to promote party unity at a time when party unity was thought to be essential. It was not surprising, there-fore, that the Executive agreed on a form of consultation within the Party which would be phrased in a way that was most likely to accentuate Lord Home's strengths. Thus, Members of the Party in the House of Commons and the Lords would be asked to give not only their first preference, but also their second preferences. They were also to be asked whether they felt particularly opposed to any of the four candidates. It was expected that Lord Home would do particularly well on the second preference, and that few Members would express any opposition to him. The formal consultation would also be carried out by men who knew that 'the back-bench Cabinet' had plumped decisively for Lord Home.

When the leadership issue had arisen in 1957, the effective decision had been taken by the Cabinet without reference to the 1922 Committee. But even if Harold Macmillan had been anxious to have his successor chosen in the same way, it is doubtful whether the procedure adopted in 1957 would have worked so quickly and so well in 1963. There were too many candidates. A multiple choice had created a partial political vacuum, and under John Morrison's leadership, the 1922 Com-mittee Executive had the confidence to step forward and fill it.

Of course, Cabinet Ministers did not relinquish all interest in the question of the succession. Iain Macleod and Enoch Powell in particular were busy rallying support for Rab Butler. At the time, there were some who criticised Rab Butler for not fighting harder to promote his own candidature. But they were not aware that John Morrison had gone out of his way to warn Rab Butler that 'The chaps won't have you'. It had not been a warning that was meant to be taken lightly – and it was not.

The original minutes for the meeting on 25 July, 1963, had read – 'The Prime Minister, who received a warm welcome, spoke to the Committee and answered questions'. These had to be amended by the Chairman, who added – 'Mr Macmillan' after Prime Minister – for the Prime Minister 'who received a standing ovation' at the next meeting on 14 November was Sir Alec Douglas Home. It was the only occasion on which the Committee was addressed by a Prime Minister who was not a Member of either the Lords or the Commons, for Sir Alec had renounced his title as 14th Earl of Home but had not yet been returned as the Member for Kinross at the by-election which was under way. As Secretary of State for Commonwealth Relations and Leader of the House of Lords, he had last come to the Committee in April 1960, when fears about immigration were beginning to stir, and there was still a sprinkling of Members present who could remember the notable contributions he had made in the Committee as Lord Dunglass before the 1945 General Election.

1964 was bound to be an election year, and for some time voices had been raised in the Committee asking that there should be no divisive legislation in the programme for the final session. Most of the measures which Sir Alec had discussed with the Committee when he had made his first visit on 14 November were acceptably non-provocative, but there was one glaring exception to this rule – the proposed abolition of Resale Price Maintenance – the practice, still prevalent in some fields, by which manufacturers could insist that retailers sold certain goods at a fixed price.

Many members of the party feared that the abolition of Resale Price Maintenance would put small shopkeepers at a major disadvantage in their fight for survival against department stores and supermarkets. The issue was raised by Robin Turton at the Committee's first meeting in the New Year, on 16 January,

1964, and in the following week at one of the longest meetings to be held since 1951: 'Mr Heath, Secretary of State for Industry and Regional Development and President of the Board of Trade, explained the Government's policy on Resale Price Maintenance. There was a lengthy discussion in which a number of Members took part, and Mr Heath replied to the questions and points raised at intervals.'

A contemporary record of the discussion noted that 'It was an extremely crowded meeting, and there is still obviously great disquiet about Resale Price Maintenance, although I suspect that the majority of Members have now reluctantly accepted it in principle, although they will seek to change the policy in detail. The main point of controversy will be as to whether the onus of proof should be changed:

> When Mr Heath came to the meeting, he made the point that this was a package deal dealing with monopolies, restrictive practices and mergers as well. That in an expanding economy we had to foster competition and help reduce prices wherever possible. At the moment, differences in efficiency between retailers were not passed on to consumers. The consumer should have the choice to pay more or less for the service he wants. In other countries, there has been no trouble over loss leadership. RPM would not have disappeared on its own without government action, and the other political parties would abolish it at one fell stroke. Our proposals were infinitely fairer as until the Court had decided in the case of a particular industry, the practice would continue.
>
> There was almost unanimous criticism of the Government's proposals on the ground of timing. Members appeared almost equally divided on the merits.

On 5 March, Edward Heath returned to the 1922 Committee to talk about the Government White Paper on Monopolies, Mergers and Restrictive Practices, and a fortnight later he was back again. These two meetings were divided by a brief discussion on the Royal Commission on the Trades Unions. The subjects were not unrelated for part of the criticism of the Resale Price Maintenance Bill was based on the argument that the Government was prepared to introduce legislation which might

affect its friends, the small shopkeepers, but it was not prepared
to take action to tackle the far more damaging restrictive practices enforced by the Trades Unions.

In fact the Resale Price Maintenance Bill took more of the
Committee's time during the first months of 1964 than any
single issue since the great argument about Members' pay in
1954. The 1922 Executive had one positive contribution to make
to the argument. Normally, when an important Bill is going
through the House, a Steering Committee consisting of the
Ministers responsible for the Bill, the officers of the Party Committee concerned, and one or two back-benchers with specialist
knowledge of the measure, will meet each week to discuss
amendments. At the suggestion of one of the Joint Secretaries,
the Steering Committee for the Resale Price Maintenance Bill
was substantially enlarged by the inclusion of members of the
1922 Executive to help try and hammer out a broad agreement
on various amendments before they were discussed on the floor
of the House. Exceptional measures were necessary – the famous
'chemists amendment' which would have given broad exemptions
to goods sold in chemists' shops, was defeated by one vote.

Despite the terms of the Resale Price Maintenance Bill, the
public opinion polls suggested that support for the Government
was growing, and on 23 July, the Prime Minister came to an
end-of-term meeting, which was also an end-of-the-parlia-
mentary-session. 'The Prime Minister, who was very warmly
received, addressed the Committee, and in thanking Members
for their support, spoke of the returning enthusiasm for the Party
evident in the country, and of his confidence in the final outcome
of the General Election.'

The returning enthusiasm was not quite strong enough. On
Thursday, 15 October, the Conservatives polled 12,001,396
votes and won 304 seats. This was almost exactly 1,750,000
votes and 61 seats less than in 1959. The Labour vote actually
fell by 10,000 votes from 1959 to 12,205,314 but they won 317
seats, 59 more than in 1959. The Liberals polled an extra
1,400,000 votes, but only gained three extra seats. Labour's
overall majority was four. Thirteen years of uninterrupted Conservative rule had ended.

9

Selection Rites
(1964-72)

WHEN THE 1922 COMMITTEE met for the first time after the 1964 election on Guy Fawkes Day there were no explosions and Sir Alec Douglas-Home received a standing ovation. The Party had come a great deal closer to victory than many Members had privately expected. The election campaign had clearly been fought tenaciously and skilfully, and the prospects of another General Election in the near future seemed to be good.

But Opposition was a new phenomenon for half the Members of the Committee. It would take time to make the necessary psychological adjustments. After the 1950 General Election, when the Conservative Party had narrowed the gap after five years in the wilderness, the 1922 Committee had quickly emerged as the main sounding board for attack. It had been the forum in which many loud voices had been raised with demands for all-out assault. In 1964 the Labour Government's majority was even smaller than it had been in 1950 but the areas of assault were less easy to identify in the days before the Labour Government had begun to establish a record of its own.

On 12 November Martin Redmayne answered questions about the tactical handling of debates. It was to be his last appearance before the Committee as Chief Whip. After more than four arduous years in a job that had got progressively harder as the bloom of victory had wilted he handed over to Willie White-law, the largest, loudest, jolliest, and most emotional Chief Whip that most Conservatives could remember. He was a keen golfer, and he soon showed that he could keep his ball in the centre of the Parliamentary fairway.

There also had to be a new Chairman of the 1922 Committee. After almost ten years John Morrison moved to the House of

Lords in the dissolution Honours. He was followed by Sir William Anstruther-Gray, the tenth Chairman in 41 years. He was the fourth Scotsman, the fourth old Etonian, and the first Guardsman to be elected to the Chair. Before entering the House for North Lanark in 1931 he had been seconded from the Coldstream Guards to the Shanghai Defence Force. When war broke out he rejoined his regiment and twelve years after entering the House he won a Military Cross. It was an unusual military career but Sir William's colleagues had been even more impressed by the calmness and unfailing courtesy which he had shown as Deputy Speaker from 1962 to 1964 at a time when the Labour Party had tasted blood, and the Chair had frequently come under fire in a whole series of rowdy debates.

At the Committee meeting after Sir William's election and when Willie Whitelaw made his debut as Chief Whip, Selwyn Lloyd opened another discussion on party tactics in the course of which 'the Chief Whip requested Members not to ask the Government Whip's Office to find them a pair as this was playing directly into their hands'. But it was still the Conservative rather than the Labour record which was under the heaviest attack and at the last meeting before Christmas Reggie Maudling came to the Committee to talk about the current financial position and, incidentally, to advise Members how they might best meet the charge that the Conservatives had left their successors a deficit on the balance of payments of £800 million in one year.

The first meeting of the Committee in 1965 coincided with polling day at the Leyton by-election – an election that was held as the local Member had been moved to the House of Lords in order to provide a safe seat for Patrick Gordon-Walker who had been appointed Foreign Secretary, despite his defeat at Smethwick at the General Election. When John Harvey, the Member for the neighbouring seat of Walthamstow East, reported that the Conservative candidate at Leyton stood an excellent chance of winning the seat and appealed for volunteers from the 1922 Committee to go straight down and do some last-minute knocking-up of supporters who had not yet voted, he was greeted with happy but ironic laughter.

On Thursday, 4 February, 1965, the Chairman welcomed to the Committee Ronald Buxton, the unexpected victor of Leyton.

It had been a notable success which put fresh heart into the Committee; and it provided the best possible setting for Ted Heath's first report on the work of the Party Policy Groups. He could tell the Committee that Sir Alec was giving unprecedented encouragement to the development and preparation of detailed policies. The Leyton by-election had shown that these groups would have to work even harder and faster than had first been imagined.

Meanwhile Sir Alec had been working on a detailed policy statement that only he could make. Both before and after the choice of Sir Alec as Leader there had been criticism of the procedures used. In 1957 the Cabinet had made the choice of Leader. In 1963 the political realities made it difficult for the Cabinet alone to decide and an unrecorded and largely unknown meeting of the 1922 Executive had a decisive influence on the selection procedures, and thus on the selection itself. In the event, more people had been consulted than ever before but it had not been immediately clear what weight had been given to the advice received. In a celebrated critique of the 1963 selection process which he contributed to *The Spectator* on 17 January, 1964, Iain Macleod had argued 'the procedure which had been adopted opens up big issues for decision in the future ... I do not think it is a precedent that will be followed.'

On 25 February Sir Alec came to the 1922 Committee and announced his decision on the procedure to be followed in future for the selection of a new Leader for the Party. The new Leader would be elected by Conservative (and National Liberal) Members of Parliament and the machinery would be presided over by the Chairman of the 1922 Committee.

The detailed plan proposed

(1) There shall be a ballot of the party in the House of Commons.

(2) The Chairman of the 1922 Committee will be responsible for the conduct of the ballot and will settle all matters in relation thereto.

NOMINATIONS AND PREPARATION OF THE BALLOT

(3) Candidates will be proposed and seconded in writing. The Chairman of the 1922 Committee and a body of scrutineers designated by him will be available to receive

nominations. Each candidate will indicate on the nomination paper that he is prepared to accept nomination, and no candidate will accept more than one nomination.

The names of the proposer and seconder will not be published and will remain confidential to the scrutineers. Nominations will close 24 hours before the first and second ballots. Valid nominations will be published.

(4) The scrutineers will prepare a ballot paper listing the names of the candidates and give a copy to each voter at a meeting called by the Chairman of the 1922 Committee for the purpose of balloting and consisting of all Members of the House of Commons in receipt of the Conservative and National Liberal Whips.

FIRST BALLOT

(5) For the first ballot each voter will indicate one choice from the candidates listed, and hand the ballot paper to the scrutineers, who will count the votes.

(6) If as a result of this ballot one candidate *both* (i) receives an overall majority *and* (ii) receives 15 per cent more of the votes cast than any other candidate he will be elected.

(7) The scrutineers will announce the number of votes received by each candidate, and if no candidate satisfies these conditions a second ballot will be held.

SECOND BALLOT

(8) The second ballot will be held not less than two days and not more than four days after the first ballot, excluding Saturdays and Sundays. Nominations made for the first ballot will be void and new nominations, under the same procedure as for the first ballot, will be submitted for the original candidates, if required and for any other candidate.

(9) The voting procedure for the second ballot will be the same as for the first, save that paragraph 6 above shall not apply. If as a result of this second ballot one candidate receives an overall majority he will be elected.

THIRD BALLOT

(10) If no candidate receives an overall majority, the

three candidates receiving the highest number of votes at the second ballot will be placed on a ballot paper for a third and final ballot.

(11) For the final ballot each voter must indicate two preferences among the three candidates by placing the figure '1' opposite the name of his preferred candidate and the figure '2' opposite the name of his second choice.

(12) The scrutineers will proceed to add the number of first preference votes received by each candidate, eliminate the candidate with the lowest number of first preference votes and redistribute the votes of those giving him as their first preference among the two remaining candidates in accordance with their second preference. The result of this final count will be an overall majority for one candidate and he will be elected.

PARTY MEETING

(13) The candidate thus elected by the Commons Party will be presented for election as Party Leader to the party meeting constituted as at present.

All the old arguments that it would be unwise to give an exactly equal vote in choosing a potential Prime Minister to a senior Cabinet Minister and to the newest recruit to the Parliamentary Party had been swept aside. Now everyone knew exactly what the rules of the game would be and the 1922 Committee was wholehearted in its support.

But after the full and enthusiastic reception accorded to Sir Alec's new procedure a certain torpor seemed to descend on the main Committee. Seven of the next twelve meetings lasted less than twenty minutes. On 15 July, 1965, the meeting lasted only sixteen minutes but in that time the Chairman was asked about reports in the press that the leadership issue had been discussed at length by the 1922 Committee Executive and that Sir Alec was contemplating resignation.

The minutes of the full Committee meeting held on Thursday, 22 July, record that 'Mr Jasper More announced the business for the following week and answered questions.

'Sir Alec Douglas-Home spoke to the Committee informing them of his intention to relinquish the leadership of the Conservative Party.'

Sir Alec's announcement was brief.

When I took over the leadership of the party in 1963 there was nothing that I could do but ask the party to fight on the ground on which we stood. Unity was too fragile and time too short for anything else.

After our narrow defeat in 1964 I knew exactly what I had to do. First to strengthen the organisation of the party and to eliminate its weaknesses. This I am satisfied is being done by Edward du Cann.

Secondly, I was determined that the party should rethink its policies to make certain that they would be up to date, and meet the needs of our countrymen who are not Socialists but who are progressive and radical. This work has been largely done and we are ready with policies either for a manifesto if there is an election or for the party conference.

The Labour Party Conference will be a bitter wrangle: ours will be full steam ahead.

Thirdly, I tried to organise our Party in Parliament so that we would present an effective Opposition. In this we have been successful.

The object of all these moves has been to turn public opinion back to the Conservatives so that we would be in a position to win a general election. You have only got to look at the results of the local elections in May and since then to see that this is happening.

I believe then that we are in a position now when a Conservative Leader can lead the party to victory at a General Election.

All that being so, I came to two promises which I have always made to you. I have always considered them binding. The first is that I would never allow disunity in the party, least of all over myself; the second, that I would tell you when I considered that the time was right to hand over the leadership to another.

The decision had to be mine and mine alone.

I have to tell you that having weighed to the best of my ability all the considerations I have asked our Chairman, Sir William Anstruther-Gray, to set in motion the new procedures. I myself set up the machinery for this change and

I myself have chosen the time to use it. It is up to you to
see that it is completed swiftly and efficiently and with
dignity and calm. I do not intend to stand for election.

It only remains to me to thank all of you for the kindness
and understanding and support which you have given to
me and my wife during these two eventful years, and to
ask you to preserve absolute unity behind the new leader
of our choice. It goes without saying that I will give him
whoever he may be my full support, at all times. Let us
now look forward to a resounding victory.

The minutes record that after Sir Alec had spoken 'Sir William
Anstruther-Gray paid a tribute to Sir Alec reminding Members
of the immense debt that was owed to Sir Alec for his leadership in bringing the Conservative Party to within a hair's breadth
of victory in 1964, and for forming the party and our policies
into a formidable Opposition.

'The Chairman announced the arrangements for nominations
and for the poll to take place on Tuesday, 27 July, and answered
questions.'

The Times political correspondent reported that

One very senior backbencher told me immediately afterwards while he was still in a state of shock that in nearly
30 years it was the ugliest and most unbearable meeting
of the 1922 Committee he had known. He said that he had
had no hint that the announcement was to come. He saw it,
in the sadness of the moment, as marking the end of an
epoch in British public life when high integrity and personal
honour counted above all else.

There is no doubt in the minds of most backbenchers
that the attempted *putsch* during the last fortnight or so
inside the Executive Committee of the 1922 Committee
clinched Sir Alec's decision to stay no longer at the top.
Sir Alec appears to have been shocked and surprised by the
weight of feeling in favour of a new man that had been
revealed inside the Executive Committee and, by implication, within the parliamentary rank and file.

In the past few days Sir Alec had been forced to recognise that he no longer had a united party behind him, nor
a completely contented one, and therefore he had to judge

what would be the best time to go. He sensed that with the leadership still in question, the party conference in October might be as unhappy as that in 1963 when Mr Macmillan resigned as leader.

As Sir Alec said at a press conference shortly after his statement to the 1922 Committee,

> No one has suggested to me that I should go. But I know that there are those who, perfectly properly, felt that a change of leadership might be right. My decision rather implies that I agree with that.
>
> You may say that I had said I hoped to lead the party into victory at the next General Election. Yes, I did, but I have to take many considerations into account ... A considerable number of people genuinely felt that perhaps another leader would be better able to win the election. I took everything into account ...

There had been no 'attempted putsch' in the accepted sense of the word, but there had been a discussion of the leadership issue in the Executive which had lasted for a long time and which had sprawled over several meetings. It had been argued that the main issues raised by Mr Wilson's Government were primarily domestic and that Sir Alec's main field of expertise lay in foreign affairs and defence, but a majority of the Executive did not want a change of leadership. Indeed it was suggested that Sir Alec's decision had been triggered not by the protracted discussion in the Executive but by the publication of a public opinion poll which suggested that a clear majority of the British electorate thought Mr Wilson was more straightforward and honest than Sir Alec. And the discussion in the 1922 Executive did coincide with the presentation to Sir Alec of some criticisms of his leadership from the Conservative Party organisation in the country.

At 11.30 a.m. on Monday, 26 July, the Chairman announced that three valid nominations for the Leadership had been received – for Mr Heath, Mr Maudling and Mr Powell.

At 11.30 a.m. on Tuesday, 27 July, the Secretaries of the 1922 Committee began to issue ballot papers in Room 14. At 2.15 p.m. Sir William Anstruther-Gray announced that the result of the first ballot was Mr Heath 150 votes, Mr Maudling 133 and Mr Powell 15.

Sir William went on to announce that a second ballot would be held in two days' time as Mr Heath had failed to secure the 15 per cent lead provided for in Sir Alec's plan. But in fact no second ballot was held. As Mr Maudling quickly announced, 'Mr Heath has an overall majority on the first ballot. I am very grateful to all the friends who have supported me, but I have no doubt at all that in the interests of the Party I should not contest another ballot.'

Mr Powell made a similar decision and when no further nominations were received Sir William announced at 11.30 on on Wednesday, 28 July, that Mr Heath was the new Leader of the Party. Just 42 years after the first Chairman of the 1922 Committee had first seen Stanley Baldwin to discuss the problem of how the new Members could learn about policy and procedure, the tenth Chairman had presided over the selection of the new Leader.

The organisation of the election of the Party Leader clearly marked one of the major events in the story of the 1922 Committee. In 42 years it had grown from being a fraction of the most junior part of the Parliamentary Party to the group that seemed to be the logical custodian of the most awe-inspiring rite in the Party's internal life – the selection of the Leader.

After the 1966 General Election, Sir William Anstruther-Gray retired as Chairman and became a Life Peer. He was succeeded by Sir Arthur Vere-Harvey. The chances of a former member of the Shanghai Defence Force being followed as Chairman of the 1922 Committee by a former Major-General in the Southern Chinese Air Force must be fairly remote, but Sir Arthur's career had been varied. After serving in the Royal Air Force from 1925 to 1930, he had become a Director of the Far East Flying Training School in Hong Kong, and two years later became 'Adviser to the Southern Chinese Air Forces'. On returning to Great Britain, he had founded the 615 County of Surrey Squadron in the Auxiliary Air Force, and had risen to the rank of Air Commodore in World War II. He had entered the House of Commons in 1945 for Macclesfield, and had subsequently acquired an impressive string of directorships in the chemical and electronic industries.

In 1970, Sir Arthur retired, and was followed in the Chair by Sir Harry Legge-Bourke, who had also been elected in 1945 – when he recorded one of the two Conservative gains at that General Election by defeating a Liberal in the Isle of Ely. While Sir Arthur's substantial scientific expertise had been deployed in commercial fields Sir Harry was Chairman of the Parliamentary and Scientific Committee and had been Chairman of the Select Committee on Science and Technology's investigation into coastal pollution after the *Torrey Canyon* disaster. At a time when the number of Conservative back-benchers with a distinctive military background was decreasing, Sir Harry was the third regular officer in succession to become Chairman of the Committee. After he had been wounded in the Greek campaign of 1941 Sir Harry became ADC to Sir Miles Lampson, the British Ambassador in Cairo. One of Sir Harry's duties involved typing the instrument of abdication which was presented to King Farouk by Sir Miles during the crisis of February 1942. Sir Harry's military background may have looked orthodox enough – Eton, Sandhurst, Royal Horse Guards – but his political career had certainly not been the stamp of ready acquiescence to established authority. In 1954, he had resigned the Party Whip in protest against the Government's policy of withdrawal in the Middle East. In the early 1960s he had been the first prominent Conservative to suggest politely that, after all the great services which the Prime Minister had rendered, the time might have come for Mr Macmillan to retire. The words that Sir Harry used are a model for those who wish to suggest that their leaders ought to abdicate. 'Men like Mr Macmillan who fought in World War I, were in politics between the two Wars, and had heavy responsibility in the Second World War, can justifiably be excused were they now to feel exhausted. It is no condemnation of those men if we should now say to them "Thank you for what you have done. Thank you for what you have tried to do. The time has come for you now to hand over this responsibility to men whose good fortune it is not to have had to bear for so many grievous years the burdens you have borne." We must all put the country first, and the country today needs unflagging vigour, undaunted hope, infallible faith and the forward look.' A military bearing did not cover any love of war for war's sake. He told the House in a moving

speech on the Common Market in October 1971, 'The House
may find it difficult to believe this, but when I was nine months
old, in February 1915, I remember my mother's brother coming
to see us before he went off to France. That was the last time
we saw him. He died of wounds in May 1915. I do not remember
my father, because he was killed in the first battle of Ypres
when I was six months old. His name is on the Menin Gate
today.'

But although the power and scope of the Committee had
changed out of all recognition in 50 years, the form and even
the content of the meetings has shown a remarkable degree of
continuity since the first days under the leadership of Sir
Gervais Rentoul.

In 1973 as in 1923, the Meetings open with the Minutes of
the previous Meeting being read and approved. In 1973 as in
1923, the Whip on duty then announces the business for the
following week, with the whipping for each day's debate, and
answers questions. In fact, it is very rare for the business on the
whipping to be changed as a result of the questions asked or
the points raised, but the Whip's announcements do provide
a regular and public point of contact with the Whips. Individual
Whips regularly attend the Party's specialist committees, but
the announcement of the whipping does provide a special,
regular attraction for the 1922 Committee itself.

In 1973 as in 1923, the Chairman calls for reports from Party
Groups. Before World War II, there were regular and even
substantial reports from the Party Specialist Committees to keep
the main body of the Party informed of any significant development. In 1972, weeks can pass without the officers of any
particular committee reporting anything at all to the 1922 Committee.

The 'reports from party groups' were of particular importance
in the early 1920s, when the whole concept of regular specialised
groups was first brought to reality by Sir Gervais Rentoul's
energy and imagination. Now, the real forum for co-ordination
and discussion of any interesting development is within the
Specialist Committees. In 1972 the chairmen of the Aviation,
Finance, Industry, Trade and Transport Committees were members of the 1922 Executive, where they sat with Vice-Chairmen
of the Defence, Foreign Affairs and Home Affairs Committees.

The idea that the Executive Committee is a sort of back-bench cabinet has some relevance as far as portfolios go.

In 1973 as in 1923, there is still the same tendency to mix the important and the trivial. In 1973, as in 1923, the subject to be discussed at the main meeting is usually decided at the last moment by the Chairman in consultation with the Executive. In 1973 as in 1923 a clear majority of meetings are not addressed by guest speakers. It is now almost unheard of for an individual who is not a Minister to come from outside the Committee to speak to it. The practice, so common in the 1930s, of inviting outside experts to address the Committee was never revived after the War, although a dozen or so more visitors will address the various Specialist Groups in the course of a normal week.

Throughout most of its existence, the Main Committee has shown a tendency to elect 'steady men whose faces have become familiar' to the Executive. Of the eighteen men elected to the Executive from the 1971-72 session only five had been Members for less than 10 years, and only one had been a Member for less than five years. Four were in their sixties, eight were in their fifties and six in their forties. Two had been regular soldiers, four were journalists, four had served overseas, three in the Foreign Office, one in the old Indian Civil Service. Three were in industry and two were in the City. For once the legal profession was under-represented, but a number of gaps were partly filled when Stratton Mills, a 39-year-old solicitor from Belfast, was elected to fill one of the vacancies caused when Cranley Onslow and Tom Boardman became Ministers. Before his election, there had been no member from Scotland, Wales or Northern Ireland on the Executive, while no less than seven members represented seats in London or the suburbs. The problem of a lack of geographical spread was particularly noticeable in the 1971-72 Executive, but it had cropped up often in the Committee's life.

But wherever the Members came from, the importance of the Executive had tended to increase over the years. As one astute Member of the Executive Committee has noted:

The meetings of the Executive who foregather in Committee Room 14, 45 minutes before the meeting of the main Committee are almost always interesting, but the meetings

of both the Executive Committee and the main Committee
only become important when the Party is going through a
bad patch. When everything is going well, Ministers or
Shadow Ministers can ignore the views of the 1922 Committee with impunity, but if there is trouble a firm reaction
from the 1922 can be vital.

The 1922 Committee was not very keen on the policy
of retreat from Africa, but when Harold Macmillan was
at the top of his powers, he would give us a lecture about
Norman land-holdings in Saxon Britain and that would be
that. But when political stormclouds blow up, the Executive
could not be sent away with historical lectures. We matter
intermittently.

Obviously, the views of the 1922 Committee are more important when the issues are of medium rank. Even if it wanted to,
the 1922 Committee could not reverse a Conservative Government's decision to withdraw from Africa, but it could push a
Conservative Government into breaking the BBC's monopoly
of television. The 1922 Committee could not force a Conservative Government into dropping or postponing the Resale Price
Maintenance Bill, for that might have meant the overthrow of
the Government, but it could push a coalition Government into
dropping its fuel rationing scheme in the middle of a war. Clearly
the 1922 Committee can operate most decisively in those issues
where the existence of a Conservative Government is not at risk.

Two points stand out. First, when one considers the vast
range of issues in modern politics, the number of occasions on
which there has been head-on conflict between Ministers and
back-benchers is really remarkably small and says much for the
easy give and take exercised by Governments and back-benchers
in the past 50 years.

Secondly, when one does look at the issues which have
produced friction, the back-benchers have been right at least as
often as the Government. To take but two examples, in 1944
and 1945, the 1922 Committee's views of what was happening
in Poland and Eastern Europe as a whole was much more
realistic than the official line advanced by Foreign Office

Ministers, while the views expressed by the Committee in the early 1960s on the desirability of controlling Irish immigration would command even wider support in the early 1970s.

As one Member put it, 'When it is working well, the 1922 Committee is the conscience of the Party. If the Government is leading a righteous life, we will not bother it, but a Government or a person who has a continually troublesome conscience will not be much good. On the other hand, a weak conscience is no good to anyone. It is no exaggeration to say that if the 1922 Committee does not have a strong, independent existence of its own, the Party as a whole will suffer.'

As Sir Harry Legge-Bourne noted shortly before ill-health forced him to relinquish the Committee chairmanship on the eve of the Committee's 50th birthday:

Generally the Executive do not wish to enter into dispute with their Leader. Their object is rather to convey to him matters of great concern to the Party, or to hear from him views and proposals which he would like to test as to their likely effect upon the Party, before final decisions are taken.

The traditional right, therefore, of the Chairman of the 1922 Committee to seek audience with the Leader of the Party is one that it is wise to use sparingly. If, every other day, the Chairman were to seek an audience with his Leader, inevitably the importance of the occasion would be diminished by familiarity and excessive frequency. It is only on great issues that these meetings are arranged, and even then much will depend upon the relationship of the Chairman and the Chief Whip of the day. The closer the Chairman and the Chief Whip keep in touch with each other, the less likely it is that the Leader will have to be brought into such discussions, although however close the Chief Whip and the Chairman of the 1922 may be, the Chairman always has to remember that the 1922 Committee is not a disciplinary body. It is the central forum of the Parliamentary Party on the Back Benches, and for this reason, the Chairman has to be careful never to become what might be described as a 'Whip's Man', or indeed as a 'Prime

Minister's Man' or a 'Leader of the Party's Man'. He has always to remember that his first duty is to the 1922 Committee itself.

Inevitably, much depends upon each Chairman being able to judge the type of men with whom he is dealing, and to adjust his presentation of the 1922's attitudes accordingly. Some Prime Ministers have been forthcoming, and ready to answer any questions fired at them by any Members of the Executive at the meetings which they attend. Others will listen. Some perhaps forget what they are told. Others have memories superior to that of the elephant, and never forget. Some form quick judgements, others reserve the right to contemplate what is said before making up their minds. This inevitably places upon the Chairman of the 1922 Committee the burden of ensuring that when he takes the Executive to see the Leader of the Party, the case is presented in a way most likely to appeal to the type of man their Leader is.

But the work of the Chairman has many other facets. Each week the Executive meets some three-quarters of an hour before the main Committee meeting on Thursday evenings; and although the Chairman may think that in one week he has cleared the decks of all the matters he would like to raise with his Executive, by the time the next Thursday comes along, all too often he has to present them with an agenda of such urgency or so complex that it is difficult to complete the business within three-quarters of an hour.

Indeed much of the most important work of the 1922 Committee is done at these Executive meetings, and sometimes a very deep searching discussion on policy may take place in the Executive, only to be followed by a brief and sometimes pedestrian meeting of the main Committee at which no important issues are raised at all. In the middle of one grave international crisis, the 1922 preferred to discuss the alleged inadequacies of the Kitchen Committee!

As the week goes by between each meeting of the 1922 Committee, the Chairman and other Members of the Executive will be approached by Members on certain issues which they may be contemplating asking to raise in the main Committee. Sometimes, after discussion, they decide that discretion is the better part of valour, or that the information which either the Chairman or Members of the Executive are able to give satisfies them sufficiently to make them feel it no longer is necessary to raise the matter in the full Committee.

The job of Chairman is not entirely confined to the House of Commons. One of his duties is to maintain a weekly link with the Independent Unionist Peers, who are the House of Lords' Conservative equivalent of the 1922 Committee. They meet earlier on Thursday afternoons. There is also a weekly meeting in Central Office at which the current political situation, not only in Parliament, but also in the country, is considered with the Chairman of the Party Organisation presiding.

Periodically, also, the Policy Advisory Committee meets. This brings in Conservatives from Central Office, the Areas, and the various Advisory Committees, as well as Young Conservatives and Conservative Students.

The National Union of Conservative and Unionist Associations is the central pillar of the Party organisation in the country, and there are three Committees of this Organisation which the Chairman and selected additional Members from the 1922 Committee are entitled to attend. These are the National Executive of the National Union, the Finance and General Purposes Committee, and the Sub-Committee which is specially set up to select the resolutions for discussion at the Party Conference each year. A recent decision has led to the Chairman of the 1922 Committee also being appointed to serve on the Standing Advisory Committee on Candidates for General Elections.

These Committees and Groups all involve often considerable paperwork for the Chairman of the 1922 Committee. Indeed, the job might almost be described as a Christmas Tree – so many other things are hung upon it. The central stem of that tree is the very special relationship which the Chairman hopes to be able to enjoy with every Member. When great issues, as for example Suez or, in more recent times, the Common Market, are tending to divide the Party, one of the most important roles of the Chairman of the '22 is to try to ensure that at the end of the day, however acrimonious the discussions may have been, everyone is still glad to talk to everyone else.

To be chosen by one's colleagues to be their Chairman is a very delightful privilege, but it carries with it the demand for great humility as well as dedication. Looking down the list since 1945, Sir Arnold Gridley, Sir Derek Walker-Smith, Major John Morrison, Sir William Anstruther-Gray, and Sir Arthur Vere-Harvey, one inevitably compares each with the others, and tries to pick out the particular examples each of them set which one would like to be able to emulate. A capacity to steady the Party when morale was low was never better shown than it was by Sir Arnold. The expression of the Party's views was rarely more cogently expressed than in the days of Derek Walker-Smith, whose phraseology ideally matched that of Winston Churchill. The capacity to judge how best to handle the affairs of the Committee under two Prime Ministers so diametrically different as Sir Anthony Eden and Mr Harold Macmillan showed the true genius of Major John Morrison. Sir William Anstruther-Gray's abounding kindliness was something which was entirely infectious and lovable. And Sir Arthur Vere-Harvey perhaps did more than any of his predecessors as Chairman of the 1922 to lay foundations for a closer association between the Area Chairmen, the National Union and the Parliamentary Party.

'True patriotism does not consist of loyalty to one's country as it is, but to a conception of what we would like it to become'.[*] So it is with Party loyalty. No Party can afford to stand still. The 1922 Committee's greatest strength lies in its ability to conserve that which is good, to discard that which is no longer relevant, and always to be aware of how much the future of the Parliamentary Party, and its ability to tackle the problems which will confront their successors, depends upon the Committee keeping its eye not on current affairs but also on the political horizon.

> Time past and time future
> What might have been and what has been
> Point to one end, which is always present.[†]

[*] J. William Fulbright, *The Arrogance of Power* (Random House 1967).
[†] T. S. Eliot 'Burnt Norton'.

At the annual luncheon given by the 1922 Committee to the Prime Minister in 1971, he was reminded of some words which he had used in his own maiden speech on 26 June, 1950: 'Magnanimity in politics is not seldom the truest wisdom.'

That the Conservative Party has so successfully triumphed despite the stresses and strains of the past half-century, and is now in power, is in no small part due to the magnanimity which has moderated the 1922 Committee.

The honourable record unfolded in this book has depended to an incalculable degree upon that magnanimity being maintained between the Leadership, the Whip's Office, the Chairman, the Officers and the Executive and every Member of the 1922 Committee. May it continue to flourish! For without it, not only the Party, not only the House of Commons, but also the Nation itself would be the poorer.

INDEX